JUST ADD WATER

JUST ADD WATER

YOUR GUIDE TO THE ULTIMATE CRUISE VACATION

ROB & KERRI STUART

Copyright © 2014 by Rob and Kerri Stuart
All rights reserved. In accordance with the U.S. Copyright Act of 1976, the scanning, uploading, and electronic sharing of any part of this book without the permission of the publisher is unlawful piracy and theft of the authors' intellectual property. If you would like to use material from this book (other than for review purposes), prior writer permission must be obtained by contacting the publisher at permissions@theleveragecompany.com.
Thank you for your support of the authors' rights.

Although every precaution has been taken to verify the accuracy of the information contained herein, the author and publisher assume no responsibility for any errors or omissions. No liability is assumed for damages that may result from the use of information contained within.

Designations used by companies to distinguish their products are often claimed as trademarks. All brand names and product names used in this book are trade names, service marks, trademarks or registered trademarks of their respective owners. At the time of publishing, the authors disclose they have received travel industry discounts to sail aboard some of the cruise lines listed and discussed in this book.

Editor: Stephen Hirst
Cover Design: Shake Creative, www.ShakeTampa.com
Inside Layout: Forget Me Not Creative, Inc.

Printed in the United States of America
FIRST EDITION.
ISBN: 978-0-9908065-0-9
Library of Congress 2014916399

Published by The Leverage Company USA, L.L.C.

10 9 8 7 6 5 4 3

DEDICATION

ROB

First, I would like to thank my mom, Barbara, who got me started in the 1st grade reading the Hardy Boy / Nancy Drew mysteries. My love of books has never stopped!

Second, I would like to thank my gorgeous wife Kerri, who is not only the reason I started and fell in love with cruising, but without her, this book and the great stories within, would never have happened.

KERRI

I would like to thank my brilliant and funny husband Rob, since he is the one writing this dedication. He truly is amazing and there is no one I'd rather be with and travel the world. Oh, and my parents Ken and Ginny, who have always supported my independence and adventurous spirit.

ACKNOWLEGEMENTS

To our business partner and star of the hit ABC show *Shark Tank*, Kevin Harrington. Thank you for always being there for us as both a friend and a trusted business advisor.

Special thanks to Daniel Priestly, Topher Morrison, Jodi McLean and Mandi Foster from Key Person of Influence.

A huge thank you to our editor Stephen Hirst who took our words and made them sound even better. And to Gabe Aluisy who made our cover look killer and provided some great author insights along the way.

And most of all, THANK YOU to our friends, family and clients who trust us to help guide and plan their cruise vacations. Nothing makes us happier than seeing pictures of your smiling faces when you come back from your cruise.

TABLE OF CONTENTS

WELCOME ABOARD 1

WHY TAKE A CRUISE? 15

TOP 7 CRUISE MISTAKES 29

WHY YOU NEED A TRAVEL AGENT 35

HOW TO CHOOSE THE RIGHT CRUISE LINE AND SHIP 47

WHERE CAN I GO? 81

KNOW BEFORE YOU GO 95

LIFE ONBOARD 113

PLACES TO SEE AND THINGS TO BUY 145

GROUP & THEME CRUISES 151

RIVER CRUISING 161

SOCIAL MEDIA & STAYING CONNECTED 171

7 NIGHTS, 7 TIPS, $700 IN SAVINGS..175

BON VOYAGE.. 181

AUTHORS.. 185

ALL ABOARD TV..187

Travel Agent Contact Info:

_____
Name

_____
Email

_____
Phone Number

INTRODUCTION

WELCOME ABOARD

"THE WORLD IS A BOOK, AND THOSE WHO DON'T TRAVEL ONLY READ ONE PAGE." -ST AUGUSTINE

Where do you want to go? Or to quote a famous line, "Where would YOU rather be?" Think about it. Right now. Someone hands you $10,000 and you can only use it on a vacation. And you have to go soon. Now, if you are like most people, I bet you already have a place in mind! Some people call it a bucket list. We call it our "to do" list. Most likely, you know when you want to go, where in the world and who you will bring with you. Write your answer here, right in this book! Seriously, grab a pen. Unless this is not your book, or you have not purchased this yet. Then again you may be reading this on an iPad. DO NOT write on the iPad!

I am going to travel to:

_____
(Destination or Country)

I am going to visit:

_____
(cities, monuments, historical places, beaches, etc)

I am going by this date:

_____
(Month, Date, Year)

The odds are that wherever you picked, you can get there by taking a cruise. Or at least get close, and take a shore excursion. The information in this book will help you realize your goal. Not only can you see the world while traveling on a cruise ship, you will soon learn it is the easiest, safest and most enjoyable way to experience the world. And along the way, we will give you some tips and ideas that will save you $500 to $1000 or more per cruise, which can add up to tens of thousands of dollars over the course of your cruise career.

How It All Began

It was huge. Bigger than I thought it would be. Pulling in to the port of Seattle, I could not believe how big the ship looked.

JUST ADD WATER

My first ever cruise, and I had absolutely no idea what to expect. As we pulled closer to the Holland America *ms Oosterdam*, I thought to myself, "How many people can they fit on this ship?" As it turned out... a lot: over 2600 passengers and crew. I had never even heard of Holland America, and it took me a few attempts to figure out how to pronounce the name of the ship (Oh-ster-dam).

It was 2005, and I was dating a girl named Kerri, who would eventually become my wife. Ever since I was a young boy growing up on the mean streets of St. Louis, (all right, middle class home with nice streets) I always had this idea that the first girl to ask me to go on a cruise would be the girl I would marry. OK not really, but I DID see all the women that threw themselves at Doc on *The Love Boat*, and thought, "hmm...that could be a fun way to travel...anyway. A lot of people who have never cruised think it IS just like *The Love Boat*. And in some ways it is, but in most ways it's not.

Kerri had been asked by a client to join them on an Alaskan cruise to video the winners of an incentive trip (no, I was not a winner). Even though I had lived in Tampa for eight years, I don't even think I had seen a cruise ship, and am almost 100% sure I had never set foot on the deck of one.

ROB & KERRI STUART

Her travel was covered, so for the cost of a plane ticket to Seattle I got to tag along on a seven day Alaskan cruise. Little did I know how much that decision would affect the rest of our lives. It inspired us to become travel agents—specifically, for the cruise industry. We even partnered with one of the stars from the hit TV Show *Shark Tank*, Kevin Harrington, to executive produce our cruise show, *All Aboard TV*. And it was all because of a great experience on a cruise ship.

I saw the *Oosterdam* as we approached the port in Seattle, and if you have ever seen a cruise ship up close, you know it's a breathtaking sight. To this day, it's still one of my favorite things… to see the ship (or ships) as you pull into the port area. People getting off the ship, people waiting to get on, supplies being loaded. There was no way to predict that this first cruise would ignite—whoops, bad cruise word— "turn into" a passion that would become our profession.

Walking onboard the ship was an incredible experience: cruise newbies standing around, gaping in awe at the sheer scale of the ship; experienced cruisers navigating around them angling for the buffet on the top deck; families craning their necks around, searching for their cabins. For the first few hours we just walked around with our mouths open.

JUST ADD WATER

You can actually feel the excitement in the air as the ship gets underway. There were no crowds standing on the dock waving to us as we left like you see on TV and in the movies, but we wouldn't have noticed anyway.

We left Seattle and cruised north past mountains and glaciers so majestic that even video can't possibly do it justice. You have to "just go away." Go there in person…bring your camera for pictures AND video (and by camera I mean smart phone). We even recommend binoculars, especially on an Alaskan cruise.

Everyone on the ship was constantly on the look-out for whales, and you never knew when they would suddenly surface off the side of the ship. The captain and crew were quick to help point out wildlife, glaciers and picturesque places that were all around us throughout the trip.

We visited cities like Juneau, Ketchikan, and Sitka, surrounded by people that were just glad to be there. Still one of my many favorite things is seeing people having fun on a cruise.

Since this was also Kerri's first cruise, we had a blast, partly because we had no idea what to expect. Everything we saw or did was a first for us, making it a very memorable experience.

In hindsight, however, we wish we would have been better prepared. Maybe had a book like this one.

Even though Kerri was working, we had plenty of free time. We took some pictures, but did not have our own video camera. Man, how I wish we had had iPhones back then. And this was a little before Facebook or Twitter— no one even knew the term "Social Media." People had to wait to see pictures until after the trip. Now you can post, tweet, upload and pin pictures and video before you even leave the dock. Live streaming vacations!

We made last minute shore plans, just went with the flow of the group and really, just stood in awe of this amazing way to see a new part of the world. Why hadn't we done this before?

After that incredible cruise, we would often sit at the pool on weekends with a stack of cruise brochures and a few adult beverages, reading and dreaming of a way we could cruise all over the world. How we would visit Italy, the islands of Greece, travel through the heart of Europe on a river cruise, visit China, the Far East, Antarctica…we were even curious about what cruising on a Disney ship would be like. There didn't seem to be a place in the world that wasn't reachable somehow by a cruise ship. We read about cruises that were 30 days…60 days…around

JUST ADD WATER

the world…who gets to do this? How can they get the time off? Still, what a goal!

A few years and a few cruises later, when we were planning our wedding, we both agreed a cruise would be the perfect way to get married. OK…she would have been happy to elope, but that would have made more than a few people mad (including me, her parents and my mom).

The BIG day: October 1, 2009. We got married on the *Carnival Inspiration*, surrounded by family and friends, as it was docked at Port Tampa Bay. Guests were invited to attend the ceremony and reception on the ship while in port, or they could travel with us for our four-day wedding cruise to Cozumel, Mexico. It was the perfect combo, and while we had about 70 people at our wedding, a good 20 sailed with us, which made the entire weekend a fun celebration with friends and family. The ones who sailed with us still talk about it to this day!

When the subject comes up, I still tell people that it's the best and easiest way to get married. The crew at Carnival did a fantastic job! All we had to do was show up, and get dressed in our wedding duds. Oh, and my buddies made me do a few shots—of what, I can't even remember. It was even fun to see our friends who weren't cruising "explore" the ship while waiting for the wedding to start. It's just cool to be standing on the deck of a cruise ship. If you have cruised before, you know.

And being a wedding couple on the cruise ship had its perks, from free drinks sent over by other cruise passengers who we didn't know, to being the official "newest newlyweds" on the entire ship—which apparently is a pretty cool thing (the couple that got married 30 minutes before us wasn't too happy about it—they missed out on being in the "Couple's Game Show" on stage in the main theater).

After being back home for only a week or so, and recovering, we flew to Italy for our honeymoon aboard the newly christened Carnival Dream on its third voyage, a 12-night sailing from Civitavecchia (the port near Rome). Talk about that "new ship" smell!

Here is just a quick sample of what we did on this amazing honeymoon. We traveled to Naples, saw the canals of Venice, walked the walled city of Dubrovnik (Croatia), hung out in Sicily, almost made it to Barcelona (you'll read more about that later), enjoyed an amazing overnight experience in Monaco and then climbed to the top of the famous leaning tower of Pisa after disembarking in Livorno (the port for Florence and Pisa). Not to mention, we did a little pre- and post- cruise stay to enjoy a few

JUST ADD WATER

more days in Florence and Rome. This is definitely a dream trip. If you have to choose only one itinerary in the Mediterranean, make sure this is at the top of the list!

A year later on Oct 1 2010, we sailed again on the *Carnival Inspiration* for our 1st anniversary. I even have the shirt to prove it. What a year!

It's probably no surprise that my wife and I decided to turn our passion for cruising into our full time business. I had no idea that there were so many different cruise lines. Most people can name five or six, but there are actually over 30 cruise lines, all offering something different.

The stories we share in this book aren't to brag about the places we have been to. They are meant to inspire you to go and explore the world. We realized once we went on our first cruise that there is so much to see, and we were determined to see it. Since our first cruise we have sailed the three main cruise regions of the world: Caribbean, Mediterranean and Alaska. We have been on over a dozen different cruise lines, some more than once, and have seen firsthand the differences between what each cruise line has to offer to its guests and what to expect. There is a cruise line for every budget and every type of traveler.

Our goal is to turn your "I've always dreamed of going there" into "I can't wait to go back!"

I hope you read this book and say "I'm going!" Heck, take us with you via this book. Take a picture of you holding this book at a distant port of call and email it to me. You can do that here: Rob@AllAboardTV.com. Maybe we'll even show that picture on our TV show.

Get Off the Couch...Out of the House...GO THERE!

It's our opinion that those who travel the world, as opposed to just reading about it or seeing it on TV, are the smartest, most educated people we know. And I don't mean book smart—there is no substitute for seeing things up close and in person. Gazing at structures over 2000 years old, seeing cultures and architecture that haven't changed much in centuries, walking on cobblestone streets built by the Romans, visiting UNESCO World Heritage sites. Witnessing with your own eyes the iconic temples and monuments of Ancient Greece, or the Great Wall of China. You get the idea. Exploring these places in person will give you an entirely different perspective on things, no matter where you come from, or where you live.

JUST ADD WATER

Lucky for us, and for you, we know how to use a cruise ship as the way to visit places all over the world. You can start with baby steps by going on a Caribbean cruise and visiting a few islands. You will quickly get comfortable and realize that your goal to go to Italy and see the amazing sites built by the Roman Empire is not only in reach, but you can be confident because you are traveling on a cruise ship. You know the tips and tricks, what to expect, and most of all, you have this book to help you plan an amazing cruise.

Use This Book

Read it, highlight, take notes, dog ear some pages. This is not a book to be left on the shelf. Take it on the trip with you. Take notes in the back of this book. We have space for you to do that. Well, unless it's not yours.

Disclaimer

To begin with, I am not politically correct. So it makes sense that this book is not either. I know that probably won't offend you. My editor had to delete a few words that some people "may find offensive." If you are used to staying at the Waldorf and experiencing five-star service, then I will say that Carnival may not be the brand for you. And as you have already learned, we love Carnival. If you ARE used to Waldorf/Ritz type of service, don't worry. We've got you covered with multiple cruise lines.

We will give you direct and un-biased information when we have been there, and the best possible, researched information when we have not. If that's OK with you, then let's cruise.

If you can afford a vacation, then you can afford a cruise. Even if you don't think that you can afford a vacation, don't worry. *Just Add Water* will show you how to pay for a cruise over time, with no interest.

If you have a travel agent and they are only online, a small "roaming" gnome, or a certain TV actor from a 1960's science fiction show, you NEED this book! You will learn the importance of a real travel agent, and one that specializes in cruises. As you will soon see, there is A LOT to know when it comes to this niche market, and as a cruise specialist I can attest to the fact that there is always something new to learn. If I had to add land vacations and resorts to the list, my head would explode! But I do have partners that specialize in those!

JUST ADD WATER

This book is designed for three basic types of people:

1. *First time cruisers* - self-explanatory.
2. *Novice cruisers* – have been on one to five cruises, usually a 3-5 day Caribbean cruise.
3. *Experienced/Frequent cruiser* – been on more than ten cruises, and usually to multiple ports throughout the world. You most likely travel on the same cruise line and may now want to expand your horizons and try out new lines, or maybe the hottest trend in cruising, river cruises. Even these seasoned travelers will find a few hidden gems in these pages.

Regardless of the type of cruiser you are, this book will help you better understand the cruising experience including:

- Where to go and when
- Choosing the right ship and cabin
- Life onboard and what to do in port
- Packing tips
- How to save money on your very next cruise
- Some real cool places and widely known world events that most people don't even know you can cruise too, like the Grand Prix of Monaco!
- Our secret, insider tips

We encourage you to bring this book along with you on your cruise. Use the notes section at the back to jot down things you liked best, etc. I am a big fan of writing things down. Travel journaling is as old as travel itself.

Who this book is NOT for: if you are a bargain shopper that always clips coupons, only goes with the lowest price on everything, and is willing to drive for 10-12 hours from your house to the port for an inside cabin…this book is probably not for you. Not that it's wrong. This book is for the people that really want to explore cruising for the optimal experiences. Most people know that you will remember seeing the incredible sites, meeting awesome people, and taking pictures that will last a lifetime, far longer than the $200 you saved by staying in an inside cabin on the lowest deck. Although I have to admit, I DO remember our first cruise with an inside cabin and since then we only sail in balconies or suites.

"I'M GLAD WE WAITED SO LONG TO TRAVEL!"
-SAID NO ONE EVER!

CHAPTER ONE
WHY TAKE A CRUISE?

If you have taken a few cruises, the answer to the above question is obvious. For the less experienced, the statistic below is telling:

> **"CRUISES HAVE A HIGHER PERCENTAGE OF SATISFIED CUSTOMERS THAN ANY OTHER VACATION EXPERIENCE" - CLIA**

CLIA stands for the Cruise Line International Association, and is the main training body for travel agents in the cruise industry. Christine Duffy, the CEO of CLIA, does an excellent job in making sure travel agents get the best and most up to date training available.

When it comes to happy customers, cruise lines are at the top. So what makes them so happy? Glad you asked.

Value

One of the most important considerations when planning a vacation of any kind is value. Regardless of whether it's for couples, a family with kids, or the fast growing segment called Multi Generational Travel (typically grandparents, parents and kids), cruising makes budgeting easy. That's because just about everything is included in the cost of the cruise: your accommodations, meals and snacks, activities, child care (or adult care for that matter; think Bingo and shuffleboard), entertainment and transportation to multiple destinations.

Many of the "big" cruise lines offer fares of less than $100 per person per night, which is much cheaper than you will find for an equivalent land vacation with a hotel room, meals, and entertainment. We even recently booked multiple clients on a seven day cruise in a balcony stateroom for only $349 per person. That's $50 a day per person! Or the same as just a one-day stay in a nice hotel with no meals or entertainment.

JUST ADD WATER

Let's take a look at a cruise out of Port Canaveral (i.e. Orlando) to a popular vacation - an Orlando theme park. For our example, we will leave out the cost to get to Orlando, as you would need to get to the port, as well, and the travel expenses would be the same. We will base the comparison on a family of four (two adults and two children).

A hotel close to Disney or Universal will most likely cost between $100 (for a three-star hotel) and $200 (for a four-star hotel). Prices get higher the closer you get to the parks. Want to stay on property at a luxury Disney resort? Expect to pay $350 to $600 plus per night. Parking is a wash because, believe it or not, most hotels close to the Orlando parks charge for parking. We hate having to pay for parking at a hotel. Just sayin'...so whether you are at the port, or at the hotel, you will pay $15-$20 per night.

Here is where it starts to tilt in favor of the cruise lines. Ticket prices average $80 - $100 per person per DAY. For a family of four, you may end up spending over $300 per day just to get IN the parks. While it's true that there are multi-day discounts that are available, they vary so much and are in such a constant state of flux that I am not even going to put in the effort to list them here. And then there's parking. Suffice it to say that it doesn't really matter which park we are talking about: Disney, Universal or Sea World. Now, if you drive to the park, expect to pay $15-$20 a day to park there too! For a seven-day trip, that's over $100 just to park at the park.

Let's talk food. Three meals a day, whether at the park or at the hotel, is not cheap. Let's assume a family of four with two kids ages eight and ten. The kids are so excited, a doughnut and a soda will keep them flying for hours. But what about you, the parents? I'm just taking a shot in the dark here, but it's a pretty good bet that if you are reading this, you are an adult. Or at least a kid who thinks his is an adult (if you are a kid reading this, please put the book down; and, by book, I mean iPad. Now go tell your parents that you really need to go on a cruise!)

Back to the food—in the parks, you will have limited options. You can do the all-day dining, but your options will be limited so you'd better get used to having the same meal everyday (ala chicken fingers and fries).

Each meal is going to run $10 - $15 per person. That's $60 -$90 a day, even if you starve the kids (which is NOT recommended). There's another $420 - $560 minimum for the week, plus the "no starving kids" clause. Let's call it an even $700 on the low end.

So where are we so far?

JUST ADD WATER

- Hotel $150 x 7 = $1050
- Parking $15 x 7 = $105
- Park admission $80 x 4 x 7days = $2240
- Meals and snacks = $700

That's easily over $4000. Don't get the wrong idea, I'm not saying don't go to Disney. My wife and I have had annual passes there for years, and we love the Mouse as much as anyone; we just don't spend a whole week there. Even as travel insiders, a week in Orlando gets very expensive. Disney is the best I have ever seen when it comes to marketing. There is something that makes people want to spend (and even overspend) when they are at one of their parks.

As I wrote this, I did a quick comparison. I found two seven-night Western Caribbean cruises from Tampa. Pricing was $1997 on one line, and $2295 on another for a family of four. They were both ocean view cabins, with the latter including an upgrade to a balcony! I also found a Miami option for $2136. Similar examples can be found for Port Canaveral and Ft Lauderdale, as well. Pretty easy to see the value so far, right? Now let's talk about how easy it is to pay for it.

Interest Free Payments Over Time!

This is one of my absolute favorite hidden gems. Let's say you find that perfect cruise, and it's 18 months away. You KNOW there is not enough money in your account to pay for it right now, and your credit cards don't have enough room on them, but it's THE cruise you have been waiting for.

Not to worry—travel agent Rob to the rescue (or Kerri; she is feeling a little left out here). In most cases, you can secure that cabin on your dream cruise for as little as $50-$100 per person, lock in the price, and be the hero in your family. Here's the beauty of it, you make payments whenever you have the money freed up—as long as you are paid in full by the final payment date. Set aside a small monthly budget. Once a month… once a quarter… after your tax refund… and here is the kicker—no interest.

But wait…what if something happens and you can't go? It's 18 months away; a lot can happen in that time. No worries— as long as you cancel 75 - 90 days out (in most cases), you can get a full refund. Just be sure when booking your cruise you understand the cancellation details from the cruise line. They do vary, so check with your travel agent.

JUST ADD WATER

Multiple Destinations - Unpack Once

We hate packing. That's why we use the best luggage, and the best travel gear and gadgets. Part of a stressful trip is the checking in and out of various hotels. Many people will take a family vacation and drive across the country, for instance, down the coast of California. In doing so, they need to stop and check in, pack/unpack every couple nights. We did a site inspection to multiple resorts one time, and over the course of a week, we stayed in three properties. We saw and experienced each one. But after that trip we both agreed on one thing — we don't know why ANYONE would want to plan a vacation to multiple places and have to haul their luggage around, and keep packing and unpacking like that. It's too much work and takes away valuable time from your vacation. On a typical seven-night cruise you can expect to go to three-five different locations. In contrast, if you were to do a seven day tour of Italy on land, you may stay in two-three different hotels. That means every other day on average you will need to pack up your suitcase, toiletries, growing amount of souvenirs, and then unpack for a couple nights. That can take you up to 60 minutes each day, or about 12 hours of your trip going through this process.

Let's compare a 12-day Mediterranean cruise with a land tour. You unpack on day one, place everything nicely in your closet and drawers and then keep it there until you leave the ship. Everything has a place and you don't have to stress about the packing and checking out process every other day. Business travelers who do shorter trips can really appreciate how nice it is to go on a trip and actually "move in" to your cabin for several days. Plus, you can also take advantage of laundry and dry cleaning services onboard. If you have a butler for your cruise (which we highly recommend), he will take care of it for you. If it were a similar land tour, way too much time would be spent dealing with luggage. You get the idea.

Safe Way to Travel

Cruising is absolutely the safest way to see other countries, especially in Europe. If you have never been to Europe, flying there is the easiest part. But once you get there, where do you go? How do you get there? And when you do get there, what do you do? Do you speak the language? Cruising takes away the fear and lets you be as adventurous as you want to be.

Our first trip to Europe was a cruise. If we didn't go there on a cruise, it would have been very intimidating. Not knowing the language and customs is the top reason most people don't go to Europe. Get over your fear! The crew on almost every cruise ship

JUST ADD WATER

speaks English, and so do the guides on the shore excursions. We were greeted by a driver upon arrival in Rome who took us to our hotel, and then picked us up the next day to take us to the cruise port. It was the same on the return home. We always felt comfortable, and the cruise lines cater to the US market.

Want to go it alone in port? Go for it. A little intimidated? Go with the group on a shore excursion. A cruise gives you the option.

Let's look at an example. You are on a Mediterranean cruise and the Leaning Tower of Pisa is on your must-see list. The port of Livorno is the closest to Pisa, but it's very industrial and not the type of place you want to hang out while waiting for a cab. It's even less fun when you don't speak Italian. And Pisa is still at least a 45-minute drive away. When you get there, you really don't know what to do. You can see the tower, but do you just go up to it and walk inside? Is it free?

Here is an alternative. Buy the Pisa shore excursion. Meet in the air-conditioned theater with fellow cruisers, some you may already know, and wait for the staff to walk you to the waiting bus. On the way, your guide gives an informative talk about the sights you'll be seeing. Once there, you can elect to stay on the guided tour, or simply wander around, buy a gelato, and enjoy the scenery.

But you can always feel safe knowing the cruise line has excursions with English-speaking guides who know where to take the group so everyone is comfortable. The ship will even hold short seminars about each port to help educate you and alert you if there are any potential challenges in the area to be aware of or to avoid altogether. Awareness is the key. Yes, there are professional pickpockets in Europe, just like there are all over cities in the U.S. Knowing this beforehand, and taking precautions, as the cruise lines encourage, will help you avoid putting yourself in that situation.

Cruising is for Everyone

Multi Gen

This is one of the fastest growing segments of travel. Multi Gen refers to adults traveling with both their kids AND their parents, and there is no better way to do that than on a cruise.

Picture this scenario: the grandparents love getting up early, and are accustomed to it. The kids love it, too. The parents? Not so much. Here is a chance for them to sleep in,

JUST ADD WATER

while the grandparents take the kids to breakfast. With today's modern cabin layouts, the kids can even do a sleepover in the grandparents' cabin. Now THAT'S a vacation (for the parents anyway). The grandparents get to spend some quality time with their grandchildren, and the parents get to relax and hit the snooze button a few times.

If you have kids along but are craving some adult conversation and want to spend some time with your parents, there are plenty of kid's programs to keep the little ones busy. And if you want alone time, send the grandparents to bingo—or the casino, if they're more into poker and slots!

The beauty of a cruise with a multi-generational family is that there is something for everyone to do. It takes the pressure off one person to feel like they need to entertain everyone in the group. You may even all plan different activities or excursions, and then just enjoy getting together at dinner to share what you did that day. A cruise works really well for large families, too. When you have a big age difference, there are activities the older end will enjoy and activities the younger end will enjoy. A ship offers both so everyone is happy and can spend their days doing what they want to do without the pressure of "having" to join mom and dad in bingo because there is nothing else to do.

Families with Kids

Want to spend every minute of your vacation with your kids? We've got your cruise. Want to see them only at breakfast, dinner and bed time? We've got your cruise. Most cruise lines have gone to great lengths to create programs that will keep the kids entertained. They aren't stupid; they know if the kids are happy, mom and dad will want to take them on a cruise again. Cruise lines even offer kids-only programs so during the day they can participate in kid-friendly activities with other cruisers their age. You get to relax and do the adult activities.

Not surprisingly, Disney is the dominant line when it comes to kids. They are so good at marketing to kids, you would think they invented them! The huge parks in California and Orlando are great feeder systems for their cruises. The Florida parks are perfect pre- and post-cruise options. If you are staying at a Disney Park, they have a bus that takes you to Port Canaveral.

Couples

A cruise really is the perfect vacation for couples—there's a reason that we got married, honeymooned and spent our first anniversary on one.

You can plan in advance as much (or as little) as you want, or just wing it once you board the ship. For dining options, you can ask for a table for two, or better yet, dine in a specialty restaurant. Guys, if you are not very good at planning (that's most of us), a cruise is the best way for your wife to see how romantic you can be. Order a bottle of champagne for the room, surprise her with a couples massage, or lie by the pool with no distractions. Indulge your inner child and go down the waterslides, try the flow-rider, climb a rock wall or simply enjoy a beautiful sunset looking out over the ocean. And guess what? The ship is doing most of the work here, so all you need to do is show up and you are the hero to your sweetheart for "planning" an amazing vacation.

Seniors

There is an old saying that cruising is for the "newlywed or nearly dead." That phrase most likely came from people who watched *The Love Boat*. Many episodes would feature an older couple, perhaps enjoying an anniversary or a younger couple honeymooning on the *Pacific Princess* (that was a real ship by the way, and was only recently retired to the scrap yard). To this day, Gavin MacLeod, also known as Captain Stubing, is still the key spokesperson for Princess Cruises. We had the honor of cruising with him on the inaugural voyage of the *Royal Princess* in Ft Lauderdale.

The number one reason why a cruise vacation is perfect for seniors is safety. They don't have to worry about going from place to place like you would on a land-based vacation. And, yes, some people (usually seniors) do live on cruises full time. They sell the house, put their belongings in storage and head to the cruise ship.

As you can see, a cruise is great for people of all ages. Now that you're ready to go, let's make sure you avoid the top seven cruise mistakes a lot of people make.

CHAPTER TWO
TOP 7 CRUISE MISTAKES

F or those of you who like short cuts, here it is. Our top seven mistakes. If you read no other chapter, at least read this one. Even what appear to be the most obvious mistakes are still made by someone every cruise. That's why all cruisers need this book.

Mistake #1 - Not Using a Travel Agent

This is the biggest mistake. When you use a travel agent (and one that specializes in cruises) you eliminate and avoid the other six mistakes. If you don't know already, using a travel agent is not only FREE, it's Gratis, On the House, costs you nothing… and yet it saves you time AND money. When going direct to the cruise lines, they will always sell you their ships, even if another cruise line would be a better choice. A cruise travel agent will find the best cruise for YOU, regardless of which cruise line it is. And, if you do prefer a particular line, she will keep an eye out for upcoming sales or specials to help save you money or bump up to a better cabin.

Mistake #2 - Choosing the Wrong Cruise Line/Ship

If you ignore the solution to the first mistake, welcome to mistake #2 (and #3 thru #7). This often happens after seeing an ad or commercial for the latest and greatest cruise ship. You are lured by the lead-in price (also known as the cheapest inside cabin) and you assume all the ships in the fleet are just as new and cool, too. They're not. Instead of relying on Facebook for cruise advice, talk to your travel agent to get an objective opinion.

Mistake #3 – No Travel Insurance

This is a HUGE mistake made by nearly all novice cruisers. If you have never been on a cruise, you don't know what to expect or what can go wrong. Flying to the port and the airline loses your luggage? Too bad. The boss tells you the week before that you have to move your vacation? So sorry. Get sick while in one of the ports? Your health insurance doesn't cover it (most likely). Are you starting to get it? Trip insurance is normally 5-6% of the total trip cost, and using a travel agent should save you enough to pay for your insurance… AND buy you a few shore excursions while on your cruise.

Mistake #4 - Not Planning Shore Excursions in Advance

Most novice cruisers assume they can choose what they want to do in port, once they are on the ship. In some cases that is OK, but in many cases the most popular excursions are already booked. If you see something you really have to do, book it before you go. (Guess who can help with that?)

Mistake #5 - Picking the Wrong Cabin

I hear it all the time from people justifying why they choose an inside cabin. "I won't be spending much time in there anyway, so who cares." If you are on a tight budget and pick an inside cabin for that reason, in some cases, your travel agent can get you in an ocean view or even a balcony for the same price. See a pattern here? The only valid reason to absolutely want an inside cabin is if sunlight is a problem because you are a vampire. Don't worry, Dracula. Even then, the curtains are pretty thick in an ocean view room.

The location of your cabin is also important. There are better places on the ship than others, some with larger balconies. Don't assume all the rooms are exactly the same. They are not.

Mistake #6 - Smuggling Alcohol

If you think that replacing a case of bottled water with vodka is being creative, try again. The cruise lines are way ahead of you. I know… vodka in bottles of water… cruise line luggage screeners take a full one-week course on how to find your booze and take it for themselves. OK, I made that up, but I did see a passenger trying to bring a case of water onboard that was taped together with duct tape! I still laugh about that one.

Want to waste time replacing your minty mouthwash with booze? Knock yourself out, they are on to that, too. How would they find that? Here's a clue: A big bottle of mouthwash lasts you four months at home. Bringing a big bottle on a 7 day cruise screams "Please Open Me I AM BOOZE." Most cruise lines now have all-inclusive drink packages that are great deals. If you want to bring a lot of your own, sail on Disney, they allow you to bring a full carry-on per person. Other lines allow for at least one bottle of wine or champagne per adult in their carry-on, (Check with your cruise line for specifics on your cruise). Corkage fees of $15 per bottle and up may apply.

Mistake #7 - Booking at the Last Minute

When it comes to cruising, "last minute" is less than 30 days from departure. The farther out you book the cruise, the better the deals and cabin selection. Book early. You can get a full refund, in most cases, if the cruise is still 90 days away or more, and you have to cancel. Or refer to mistake #3. Think you can wait and get a last minute deal? Possible, but very unlikely, especially during popular months. If you risk it, you may not go at all. If you live close to a port, and have a very flexible schedule, give it a shot. For good reason, agents are usually the first to know about last minute deals because they can let their clients know. Oh, yea… back to mistake #1.

ROB & KERRI STUART

CHAPTER THREE
WHY YOU NEED A TRAVEL AGENT

> "FOR ALL OF US, TRAVEL AGENTS ARE THE LIFEBLOOD OF OUR SUCCESS, AND IT WILL NEVER BE DIFFERENT."
> KEVIN SHEEHAN, CEO OF NORWEGIAN CRUISE LINE

I am writing this sentence while I wait to hear if a client is going to make it to her cruise on time. I always advise that customers don't fly into the port city the day of a cruise, particularly if it's cross-country. This client is a friend of a friend on the same cruise, and they were making their own flight arrangements. She called yesterday to say her flight into Vancouver didn't land until 1:15 PM. The departure time is 5:00 PM and I said that, if there are no flight issues, she should be OK. I thought she was flying in from San Francisco. NO problem. She was actually flying from Boston. Potential problem, compounded by the fact she was flying through Dallas. If I had a dollar for every time Kerri had a flight delay out of DFW, well, you get the picture.

Sure enough, bad weather in Dallas caused the incoming flight to be delayed by a few hours. It's now 2:00 PM there. Her flight is supposed to leave in 10 minutes, but not even arrive into Vancouver until 4:18 PM. Twenty minutes AFTER last call for boarding. I will write the rest of this after she lands.

* * *

As I feared, the flight landed at 4:34 PM. It did NOT make up time, as we had hoped. By the time she gathered her luggage and went through customs, the boat was pulling away, and she was still 30 minutes from the dock…learn from this mistake!

In this case, trip insurance would have covered the cost of the cruise (which was approximately $2200), plus the shore excursions of $2300, and the cost of the flight (about $1200 for two people). Travel insurance would have cost her around $500 and would have saved her thousands. As always, check with your travel agent for the actual numbers for your trip.

The end result was that I found them another cruise on a different line leaving two days after their original departure, and from Seattle instead of Vancouver. We got lucky in that Holland America had a great last minute deal on a balcony cabin. That is rare. But we still had to get them from Vancouver to Seattle. That's the value of a travel agent.

Here is another quick story to illustrate the importance of using a travel agent. I had recently booked about 50 cabins on Royal Caribbean's *Brilliance of the Seas* from Tampa for a January 2015 cruise consisting of a group of high-level business owners. They came out with a special deal that had their phone lines blowing up with 20 - 30 minute hold times, even on the agent phone number. How frustrating would that be for you as a consumer? But the deal was incredible; 50% off the 2nd person in the stateroom.

Customers had to book in May for a 2015 or 2016 sailing. Many deals like this don't include groups. This one did. Because I booked my group in late April, we were not automatically eligible. A quick (OK not so quick) call to Royal fixed that, and my clients saved money. Some of them even opted to go to a bigger cabin! Another great example of a travel agent working on your behalf.

A travel agent is not simply someone who makes the booking, takes your money, and says "thank you, call me when you want to cruise again" like many online cruise sites. (Not all online sites are like this.) They are your single point of contact for everything that happens on your trip. They are your trusted advisors and coordinators.

I am a huge fan of people who love what they do. No matter what it is that they do, they just love it and take pride in doing it well. We have all experienced that bartender or waiter who was just "over the top" good. Our guide in Florence was like that when we toured the Uffizzi Museum. He showed us 13 paintings in the whole museum and said that if he showed us any more, we would not appreciate, or even remember the ones we did see. He spent time telling us the motivation and meaning behind these paintings. He was right, and it was awesome!

For the most part, travel agents are like that. We LOVE to travel, and help others experience it. Here is an example of when we used a travel agent because of their special expertise that we didn't have.

JUST ADD WATER

Even though we booked our own cruise for our honeymoon, we used an agent for the pre- and post-cruise hotels and tours. It made all the difference. We knew cruising, but had never been to Europe. Where do we stay the night before the cruise? We wanted to see Florence and Tuscany after the cruise. Who knew that in Italian, Florence is "Firenze"? That cost us 20 minutes and a few strange looks at the train station.

We were very comfortable choosing the airfare, destination and cruise ship, but having never been to Europe, we took our own advice and used a travel agent for the rest. She picked the hotel in Rome, the excursion to the Coliseum before the cruise, took care of the transportation from the port of Civitavecchia to the train station in Rome, the train to Florence, and booked the hotel in Florence—and a few guided tours there as well. We even had a private car take us to Siena. This leads me to the main point of using a travel agent.

It's FREE!!

Recently I was speaking to a large group of very successful business owners about the benefits of a cruise vacation when I casually mentioned that, of course, working with a travel agent costs you nothing. They looked at each other as if I had spoken a foreign language. When I explained that the commission is already built into the price, even if they call the cruise line direct, several of them pulled me aside afterwards to have me look into a cruise for them. And many of these people had cruised before! Who would have thought?

Now, all of that said: as a travel agent, I still understand that there are times when travelers don't actually need one. Need to book a flight from Tampa to St. Louis, or New York to LA? Unless you don't have a computer, you probably don't need an agent for that. Want to book a hotel for a business trip in Chicago? I get it.

But if you are interested in say, an Alaskan cruise, or a European river cruise—you'd BETTER use an agent. And like many things, the question isn't "why should you use an agent?" The question is "why not?" There is no downside.

Agents who are cruise specialists take classes and study to get certifications from the Cruise Line International Association (CLIA), like ACC (Accredited Cruise Counselor) or MCC (Master Cruise Counselor). To do that, agents have to take classes, do ship inspections, book multiple cabins, and take cruises themselves. It's the same as taking college level courses for whatever it is that you do for a living. Find an agent who has one or more of these certifications, and focuses mainly on cruising. There are so many different facets of traveling that finding someone who makes it their niche will save you money and help you pick the best cruises. Looking for an-all inclusive resort in Tahiti, or a self guided tour of Rome? I'm not your guy.

Here is a quick example. If you call the cruise line direct, and get a quote that is $500 per person, and then call me…guess what? It's $500 per person, too. As stated earlier, the commissions are built into the price whether you use a travel agent or not. So going back to Mr. Sheehan's statement, it costs the cruise line more money when you use an agent. Why would he make that statement? He knows that third party endorsements are much better than saying it yourself as a representative of that company. And many people do use agents. That's why they are invited along with the media to inaugural launch cruises.

Kerri and I sailed on both the Norwegian *Breakaway* in New York City, and the *Royal Princess* in Ft Lauderdale when they launched. You can bet that we were letting our social media followers know about our private fireworks show in front of the Statue of Liberty, and meeting Gavin MacLeod, Captain Stubing from *The Love Boat*. And Gavin is one of the best cruise ambassadors the industry has.

Here is something to consider if you are going to invest your money. Do you seek advice from your buddy who went to a weekend seminar on buying stocks? Or do you go to someone that does it for a living, took specific classes and has certifications to become the expert in that area? It's the same thing with an attorney. Do you want advice from your brother who watches *Law and Order*? Or do you trust someone who has studied and passed the bar exam? It's really the same thing with a travel agent. And you don't want some jack-of-all-trades—get one that specializes in cruises. You wouldn't get a tax lawyer to handle your divorce, and it's the same with travel agents.

By the way, we're not just travel agents specializing in cruises. We are the hosts of the cruise show *All Aboard TV*. If we're not on a cruise, editing footage from our cruise show (OK, I mostly watch while Kerri does that), or researching a cruise for someone else, we're studying the industry. I get, on average, 20 - 25 emails every day from vendors and partners, and I read every word of every single one of them... well, almost. On a weekly basis, we hear about all the specials that are currently being offered, and most of them have a very short window of opportunity to act. We hear about new ships being built, and which older ones are getting a re-fit. We eat, sleep, and breathe cruising. (I know, tough life!)

JUST ADD WATER

If you have a cruise travel agent, then I congratulate you! Keep working with him and make him your best friend, stay in touch with him, take him to lunch. He will think of you first when the specials come across his desk.

If you do not have a cruise travel agent, then I would love to be your "friend in the business." I have consistently been ranked the #2 Travel Agent in my house for two years running!

With all of the new cruise ships, both ocean and river, being built each year, having a cruise travel agent on your speed dial will ensure that you know all the latest and greatest info about the industry.

Travel Agent Versus Online Booking Agency

The difference between booking with a travel agent and an online agency is the experience and the relationship. It's like the difference between buying an iPhone at the Apple store from a self-proclaimed "Apple" geek who knows, loves and is passionate about the product, and buying an iPhone from an ad on Craigslist or eBay. The product is the same, but the experience is completely different. Guess who feels better about his purchase? If you said the online guy, I'm gonna smack you.

My sister-in-law, Juli, compared it to her industry, real estate. She said "what you do for people wanting to cruise is like what I do for someone who wants to buy a house," and Juli is right! We are your trusted advisors. We have YOUR best interests at heart. We work for you!

Don't just take my word; listen to what others are saying. Here is a quote from Forbes contributor Larry Olmsted:

"The bottom line is that they know more than you do, they are better connected than you, they have access to benefits you can't get otherwise, they can often beat any other prices available (even online), and after you have planned everything, they provide a safety net during your trip that you simply won't get by booking yourself or buying insurance."

Or another from *Huffington Post*:

"Planning a cruise may sound easy, but you have to consider a lot of variables. What itinerary is right for you? Will you be spending an extra night in the departure or arrival port? Do you need to book a hotel room or car rental? What shore excursions do you want to sign up for? A travel professional can help you sort out all of the intricacies of your cruise and use their connections to secure unadvertised deals. If you're hoping to use an agent

that deals exclusively with cruise travel, you can search for one through the Cruise Lines International Association. CLIA offers an Accredited Cruise Certification for agents, which means travel professionals with this credential have gone through extensive training in order to better match travelers with the right cruise itineraries."

So what's the takeaway of this chapter? When you use a travel agent, he will save you time, you can lean on his knowledge and expertise, you have a free trusted cruise advisor, you will save money and you won't get caught up in confusing websites. Sounds good to me.

ROB & KERRI STUART

JUST ADD WATER

CHAPTER FOUR

HOW TO CHOOSE THE RIGHT CRUISE LINE AND SHIP

Choosing a cruise based on the ship vs. the destination, is almost as old as the chicken/egg debate. Everyone has their own preference, although with all the new things to do onboard, it seems to be leaning in favor of ships.

So this book doesn't turn into an encyclopedia, only a portion of the thirty plus cruise lines will be in this chapter. For your enjoyment and to keep you awake, the rest can be found on our website. Insomniacs, feel free to go there now, www.AllAboardTV.com.

Let's start with picking the cruise line. Most novice cruisers shop primarily on cost—they simply pick the cruise line that has the best price within their budget. Those same people are often surprised that when they factor in things that are included on some lines and not on the other, they can often sail on a premium line for the same cost as a mass market line. How is that even possible? It comes down to the "per day" cost. How much are you going to spend each day, regardless of the cruise line you select? When choosing a mass market line, people only look at the cost of the cruise fare, and tax. Here are a few other things to consider, and are included in some lines:

- Airfare
- Gratuities (gratuities can be $12 or more, per person per day)
- Drink Packages
- Shore Excursions
- Specialty Restaurants

A few of these items could be offered during a special sale as opposed to always part of the package.

Cruises will fall into one of two categories: ocean or river. Saltwater or fresh, you just need water (that's how we came up with our book title). Ocean-going ships are generally categorized as Mass Market, Premium and Luxury. Depending on where you look, and who you ask, these categories can often overlap. Let's

JUST ADD WATER

take a look at each, and which lines comprise them. The river cruise companies are in their own chapter, Chapter 10.

Mass Market

Mass Market ships are generally the category that most people will sail on their first cruise. They are very affordable and thus attract many guests, and open their eyes to the world of cruising. This class in ocean-going ships also offers the most ships to choose from. You are most likely familiar with these brands. Here are highlights of the top Mass Market lines.

Carnival Cruise Lines (www.carnival.com)
Carnival is by far the largest cruise line. It is most known for FUN and for its famous funnel shape and color. Carnival offers multiple ship classes: Fantasy, Triumph, Spirit, Conquest, and Dream. In addition, there is the Splendor and Sunshine but each only has one ship in its class. We have been on multiple classes and they all have something great to offer. Sadly, sometimes people take a three-day cruise on a smaller, older class ship and then assume ALL of Carnival ships are the same experience. We can tell you they are not. Any short cruise on ANY cruise line is going to attract a "booze cruise" crowd.

When a Carnival guest books a vacation, they are looking to have fun! They are known for their brand of "Fun Ships" and they certainly are. You will encounter a young, energetic demographic, although there are many guests who are in their 60s and 70s. Their ships are perfect for families with kids, multi-gen groups, and youthful adults. It is also a good brand if you have a large group you would like to put on a charter. Here are some fun facts about Carnival.

- 23 ships in their current fleet with a new ship scheduled to be delivered in the spring of 2016.

- They offer the Carnival Great Vacation Guarantee™ to US and Canadian residents on North American itineraries. In a nut shell, if you hate the cruise when you're on it, let them know and they will send you home early, plus get a refund equal to 110% of their cruise fare. Pretty cool, but we've never heard of anyone using it.

- Carnival also recently launched Carnival LIVE concert series. Think of it as an intimate concert featuring great bands aboard your ship. For a nominal fee you can attend the concert or pay more for VIP access which can include backstage pass, meet-and-greet with the band, and more. This program was launched in 2014 and thus far has received great reviews. You should check it out to see if your favorite band is on the list.

- One of the most popular additions to Carnival on some of their ships is food network star Guy Fieri's "Guy's Burger Joint." Yummers! Plus, there are also some pretty cool food options such as the Mongolian BBQ, sushi, Seaday Brunch, BBQ, pizza and more. Just be sure to check before you go which food options are available on your ship as not all ships have everything. (The steakhouse on the *Dream* was awesome – highly recommend!)

- The kids programs have been getting an update and some ships now feature Seuss at Sea and Camp Ocean.

- Other partnerships include The Punchliner, presented by George Lopez, and the Hasbro Game show, to name a few.

There is so much to learn about Carnival. They are constantly improving their brand and the experience of their guests. This is evident by the super loyal fans of Carnival. That is a result of a positive cruise experience, good service, and offering what people are looking for in a cruise vacation. We often see in Carnival Cruise fan forums people who have cruised on Carnival well over 20 times. That's a lot and there are a lot of them! And because they have so many ships and itineraries you can literally see the world from a Carnival cruise ship.

MSC Cruises (www.msccruisesusa.com)

Years ago when we were in Messina, Italy at the top of the hill looking back at all the cruise ships in port, there was this one ship that looked amazing. We would see ships from this cruise line in all the ports but had no idea who they were. We had never seen them in the US, yet on our Mediterranean cruise they were the biggest, and sometimes newest ships. Years later we heard about MSC Cruises. That was them! And yes, they are a huge leader in the cruise industry. If you are not familiar with them, you should get to know and cruise with MSC Cruises. The first time we sailed on the *MSC Divina*, we were hooked on MSC.

Here are a few facts about MSC:

- They have a fleet of 12 ships and a couple more on order. We recently saw an artist's rendering of their new ship and it looked more like a nice condo building you would see on land.

- You will find their ships year round in the Mediterranean and seasonally in the Caribbean, Northern Europe, Canary Islands, South America, Indian Ocean and South and West Africa.

JUST ADD WATER

- Their ships offer a perfect blend of Italian charm and modern elegance. We were super impressed with the overall decor of the *Divina* and felt it rivaled some of the luxury ships in the cruise industry.
- If you are a fan of Italy, you will love their Italian influence felt throughout the ship. Yes, the hand tossed Italian style pizza on *Divina* was very authentic.
- The entertainment onboard was some of the best we've ever seen. It was original, different, and first class each night. It was so good, it was often a topic at dinner.
- You will find an amazing Swarovski crystal staircase on select ships.
- The *Divina*, which is seasonal out of Miami, includes a 4D theater, an F1 simulator, and an infinity pool.
- They also have figured out how to do drink packages to give every style of drinker a great way to build their own package, as opposed to a one-size fits all beverage package.

And we can't forget the MSC Yacht Club. This club can be found aboard select ships including *Fantasia*, *Splendida*, *Divina* and *Preziosa*. Think of this club as a smaller, five-star luxury ship within a larger ship. When you book a room in the Yacht Club, the added perks are worth the expense. They include exclusive check-in where you are greeted and escorted to your suite, a team of butlers available round the clock, and spacious suites with their own Nintendo Wii consoles and large flat screen. They have a "members only" area with a panoramic view, an outdoor bar, pool and multiple hot tubs. You could easily spend your entire cruise in the Yacht Club and enjoy the complete cruise experience. It is ideal for those cruisers who want more privacy or who want to be on a large ship, yet receive the attention of smaller boutique type ships. To borrow a phrase from them, they are "The Med Way of Life."

Norwegian Cruise Line (www.ncl.com)

Get ready to "cruise like a Norwegian." You can always spot a Norwegian ship. They are the ships with the fun and colorful painted hulls. Norwegian is best known for its Freestyle Cruising concept which is eat when you want where you want. And their vast number of food options ensures you will have many choices, especially on their newest ships. They sail worldwide and have 12 ships in their fleet with another couple more on order that will be in their Breakaway Plus class, *Escape* and *Bliss*.

Norwegian is an innovator in cruising and responsible for a lot of firsts many other lines have adopted, such as:

- First to offer big-name entertainers and full Broadway productions (e.g. Blue Man Group, which was amazing!)

JUST ADD WATER

- The first private island (they have one in the Bahamas and a new one in the works down by Belize)
- First bowling alley at sea (full-size bowling, that is)
- First ice bar at sea
- First accommodations for solo travelers
- First alternative restaurant

Quite the list. Similar to MSC, they also have an upscale, exclusive, key-card-access-only area they call *The Haven*. *The Haven* is only available on select ships so check with your agent if that is your preference. Guests here have their own pool, which is in a courtyard-type area, exclusive restaurant, bar and overall place to be away from the masses on the ship.

In the last year, Norwegian has added some pretty impressive ships to its fleet. We have sailed on two of their larger ships, *Epic* and *Breakaway*. Both have over 20 dining options. We recommend if you sail on Norwegian take some time in advance to understand all your options for food and entertainment and then plan accordingly. And no, you don't pay extra at all the restaurants. There will be an up charge for some. But if it isn't in your budget, try them out or purchase one of their dining packages.

Royal Caribbean International (www.royalcaribbean.com)

Royal Caribbean is one of the top two best known cruise lines. Two words that describe RCI: innovation and imagination. You may know RCI from its HUGE ships that are often in the media or through its WOW campaign, a very fitting term for its ships and overall cruise experience. Each time they build a ship, they challenge the norm and come up with really cool features, such as a Central Park with interior facing balconies, water show at sea, robot bar and more. There is a lot to share about Royal Caribbean so, not to bore you, we will focus on some highlights and features in their fleet.

- Their fleet consists of 21 ships currently in service and five more to be added over the next four years.

- They offer the largest ship in the cruise industry, *Allure of the Seas*, which holds 5,400 passengers and is three inches longer than its sister ship, *Oasis of the Seas*. They also announced another ship that will be built and added to the Oasis class of mega ships.

- Each ship in their fleet will fall into one of seven classes – this is good to know, so if you do cruise with Royal and fall in love with a specific class, you can try all the other ships within that class, or try a ship in each class.

JUST ADD WATER

- This is the cruise line where you will find a rockwall, zipline, FlowRider® surf simulator, bumper cars, and RipCord by iFly® (sky dive simulator). They aren't on all the ships so check with your travel agent if you are interested in these activities.

- *Navigator of the Seas* and *Quantum of the Seas* are the first to offer virtual balconies in some staterooms. You'll learn more about these later in the book.

When you do book your cruise with Royal Caribbean, they have a gazillion different categories within the basic cabin categories – inside, ocean view, balcony, suite. It's best to work with your travel agent to make sure you are getting the best stateroom and to filter through all the options.

Premium

These are often the same size as some mass market ships, but offer more of a focus on personal service. The pricing is slightly higher, and they generally cater to a more experienced clientele.

Celebrity (www.celebritycruises.com)

Celebrity is owned by the same company that owns Royal Caribbean. In fact, many Royal Caribbean guests will move up to sail on Celebrity as they cruise more and want a more premium experience. Here's a little cruise trivia: the big "X" on the smokestack is the Greek letter for "Chi" from the founding family's name, Chandris. Someone told me it was supposed to be crossing spotlights like they have in Hollywood movie premiers. They were drinking at the time (OK, so was I, and I believed it).

Overall, you will feel like there are more crew members to serve you, the place settings at each meal are nicer, the shops are more upscale and the feeling is nice, relaxed and overall best described as classy. Here are a few more facts:

- They currently have 11 ships in the fleet and each ship carries between 2000 and 3000 guests except for expedition ships.

- They have partnered with Bravo to launch "Top Chef at Sea." This is a fun addition to some sailings and well received by foodies.

- If you like fine wine, they make sure to provide many options. One ship offers over 400 wines to choose from.

JUST ADD WATER

- On many of their sailings, in addition to shops, you will find special trunk shows that are often related to a part of the world you are visiting.

- Another really cool and unique store is the Innovations Store aboard three of their ships. This is an Apple store at sea. They even have Apple trained employees. Can you say DUTY FREE computer purchase?

Celebrity isn't just for couples, it's a good option for families too. They have family specific programs that combine shore excursions everyone in your family would enjoy.

Cunard (www.cunard.com)

Most people have heard of the beautiful luxury ship *Queen Mary 2*. Majestic, romantic, and classic are three words that come to mind when we think about Cunard. Cunard is primarily known for its popular transatlantic cruises between Southampton and New York. In fact, in July 2013, the *Queen Mary 2* sailed on her 200th transatlantic crossing. Fun facts about Cunard:

- Their fleet consists of three ships: *Queen Elizabeth*, *Queen Mary 2* and *Queen Victoria*, and one on order that has yet to be named.

- *Queen Mary 2*, has a kennel program onboard for its transatlantic crossings, and traveling pets get a gift bag. (How cute.)

- In addition to the popular transatlantic crossing, Cunard also offers world voyages, as well as multiple departure ports in Europe and the Mediterranean.

- Guests aboard Cunard not only get pampered in luxury, but they also can enjoy amazing libraries, world class spas, afternoon tea and many enrichment programs (that's just a fancy name for lectures).

- If you sail with Cunard, pack your dress up clothes. Not only will you experience themed balls, but there will be black tie dinners and generally guests dress up more.

- You will find well-traveled guests with a taste for nice things and a generally older crowd.

If you're thinking about heading to England for an extended vacation, why not choose to arrive or depart on an amazing Cunard ship and enjoy the journey across the pond.

JUST ADD WATER

Disney (www.disneycruises.com)

Hands down, this is the favorite for families, but it's good for adults too. Think of it as a floating Disney resort. Forget parking and long lines to get in the park. You are staying "in" the park! You will also find arguably the cleanest ships in the industry, and the fantastic service Disney is known for. Kerri and I sailed on the *Disney Magic* and it was awesome. They only have four ships in their entire fleet. So as far as supply and demand goes this also helps drive their prices up. Even at the higher prices they sell out quick.

I don't like that they don't have casinos, but that's just me wanting to play poker. I totally get why they don't—while a lot of fun, gambling simply isn't a fit for the Disney brand, which is extremely concerned about retaining their "family friendly" image.

One of the cool things about them is a concept they created called rotational dining. On a five night cruise, you will dine in three different restaurants, but with the same table mates and waiter! The perfect vacation is a stay at a Disney resort, followed by getting on the magical Disney bus for a cruise out of Port Canaveral.

Here are some fun facts about Disney Cruise Lines:

- They sail Alaska, Hawaii, the California coast, Caribbean, Panama Canal, Mediterranean and Europe (these do vary year to year).

- They were the first to have a fireworks show at sea – and, in true Disney style, they have a themed party that night.

- The details around the ship are amazing, from hidden Mickeys, and iconic drawings to decorative touches exclusive to each ship and surprise character appearances.

- They were the innovators of "virtual portholes." A virtual porthole is basically a video screen that plays what you would be seeing if you had an actual porthole to the outside. This was a great touch to help give the inside cabins a peak of the outside. And then they took it the next level and added surprise appearances by characters onto the porthole.

- They have an amazing private island in the Bahamas, Castaway Cay, and it's the only private island with its own fixed dock so you don't need to take a tender to shore.

- The design of each ship includes two red smoke stacks — similar to reflect that classic cruise liner feel. Only one is an actual working smoke stack.

JUST ADD WATER

- They received special permission from the coast guard to have lifeboats the color of Mickey's shoes – special yellow. And their hull is a rich navy color. Such a beautiful looking ship that says "Disney."

You are sure to be treated like a Prince or Princess when you cruise Disney Cruise Lines.

Holland America (www.hollandamerica.com)

The reason we love Holland America is because it was the very first cruise line we experienced. From 1873 to 1989, Holland America was a Dutch shipping line, a passenger line, a cargo line and a cruise line between the Netherlands and North America. That's quite a history. A huge part of their legacy was bringing hundreds of thousands of immigrants to North America. Pretty neat. So what else is there to know about Holland America?

- Their ships are very elegant in feel and quite spacious when compared with other cruise lines.

- Their current fleet includes 15 ships with four classes. A new class called the Pinnacle class is scheduled for release in 2016. It will feature ships that are slightly larger than their other classes.

- They are the only cruise line to offer itineraries on all seven continents with cruises ranging from 7-21 nights.

- They are the leader in Alaskan cruises and have many options to add on a land portion to your Alaskan cruise, as well.

You can find "Dancing with the Stars at Sea" onboard Holland. If you are into this show, you can take a cruise and then join dance pros and celebrities from the hit show for performances, autograph and photo op sessions, a fashion show, and more.

You will most likely find an older crowd onboard and not many kids at all. They cater to guests who have time to take longer cruises and, as a result, offer a variety of onboard activities including digital workshops, culinary arts program presented by *Food & Wine* magazine and a greenhouse spa. Their ships are mid-size ships (1,200-2,000). So, if you aren't interested in a large number of passengers onboard, you should definitely check out the cruise options Holland America offers.

Oceania (www.oceaniacruises.com)

Their tag line says it all – Your World, Your Way. You know Oceania is the right fit if these words appeal to you: sophisticated traveler, lover of world-class cuisine, enjoy personal service, enriching travel, and destination oriented experiences. Oceania Cruises offers a five-star cruising product that is exquisite, casual elegance. (How's that for a description?) When cruising with Oceania you have your choice of five vessels from their fleet representing two different sized ships. One group includes *Regatta*, *Nautica*, and *Insignia*. Each of these ships offers an intimate atmosphere with just 684 passengers and over 400 crew members. The other group of ships includes *Marina* and *Riviera*. These ships are a little larger, with a guest capacity of 1250, yet they still support their guests with a crew of 800.

Here are a few more highlights of Oceania Cruises:

- The cruise line was formed in 2002 by luxury cruise industry veterans.
- They are the world's largest upper premium cruise line.
- They sail to more than 300 ports around the globe.
- They sail to all parts of the world, including: Mediterranean, Greek Isles, South Pacific, Australia/New Zealand, Alaska, Canada/New England, Asia, Africa, South America, Caribbean, and Panama Canal. (Or you can just visit all these on a Transoceanic voyage or a Grand Voyage.)

Many who sail with Oceania Cruises will attest to it being one of the best value-for-money cruises. We were surprised to note that it is not a 100% all-inclusive line. They do offer beverage packages, unique internet packages (if you MUST stay in touch), and, if you can fly from one of their gateway cities to your departure destination, you may be able to take advantage of their Free Airfare Program. We like this latter program as it saves you the hassle of watching airfares and hoping you get the best deal.

Princess (www.princess.com)

While on a Princess cruise, we were lucky to meet TV's immortal Captain Stubing, Gavin MacLeod, from *The Love Boat*. Meeting him really felt like we were hanging out with the character he made famous. For decades he has been the spokesperson for Princess, and, if you get a chance to sail with him, do it. In fact, the cast of *The Love Boat* are the godparents of their newest ship, *Regal Princess*.

Princess is a very well known line and that show probably had something to do with it. Unfortunately, if you want to sail on that exact ship, *Pacific Princess*, it has since been decommissioned and dismantled.

JUST ADD WATER

As their current marketing campaign says, when you go on a Princess ship, you "Come Back New." We agree. In general, the decor is contemporary and elegant, nothing over the top or too showy. They best describe their ships as a small ship feel, but on a large ship.

Princess ships can be found all around the world. They offer more than 150 different itineraries and sail to six continents. They are a leader in the Alaska cruise market.

Princess has recently introduced two new ships, as well, to the market, *Royal Princess* and *Regal Princess*. This brings the total number of ships in their fleet to 17. Most of these are large ships and two that are smaller ships. The *Royal Princess* debuted in 2013, and we had a blast sailing on her. Some of the highlights included the glass-bottomed walkway, called the SkyWalk, that extends over the side of the ship. We also liked the set up of the bar on the direct opposite side that had a similar feature. And my "can't miss" on this ship is the sanctuary, an adults-only retreat at the top deck of the ship. A padded lounge chair or cabana in this area is very inexpensive and well worth it.

Luxury

Azamara Club Cruises (www.azamaraclubcruises.com)

When it comes to unique experiences at your destination with a premium cruise experience, Azamara delivers. This line is definitely more like a boutique hotel. They have just two jewel-box ships in the fleet: *Journey* and *Quest*. Each holds under 700 passengers. This cruise line's ships are basically like a floating country club. Here are some of the exclusive amenities you will enjoy.

- AzAmazing Evenings – unlike other cruise itineraries, Azamara makes a point to not only take you to some of the famous destinations, but they then kick it up about ten notches and put together an experience at a well known destination for something exclusive you will not find anywhere else.

- One very special distinction Azamara offers is the overnight stays and visits to various ports. Where most cruise lines will stop into a port just during the day, Azamara has overnights. Imagine Monaco at night. We've been there and, WOW, it's nothing like during the day.

- You will often find guest lecturers aboard who are experts in culture, history, sports and more, which can add some educational value to the destinations you will visit.

What you may not know is Azamara is actually owned by Royal Caribbean International. It was originally planned to be an expansion of Celebrity Expeditions, a sub-brand of Celebrity Cruises. However, with their distinct style and offering, it was decided they needed a line of their own.

Crystal (www.crystalcruises.com)

One of our most favorite cruise line brochures to browse through are those provided by Crystal Cruises. Think dream trips all over the world to exotic destinations. When we think of Crystal, the first word that comes to mind is luxury. Crystal Cruises consistently ranks among the top luxury properties in the world and earns top awards. What's interesting to know about Crystal is:

- Their fleet consists of two ships, *Crystal Serenity* and *Crystal Symphony*.
- You will find that about 75 percent of the guests are from the US and Canada and their travelers are very sophisticated.
- They hold some amazing enrichment classes onboard, with well-known partners such as Berlitz and Yamaha

(piano, not motorcycle). We were very impressed to see their Creative Learning Institute onboard. It's a classroom set up.

- And who can't resist cuisine by Nobu Matsuhisa and Piero Selvaggio.
- Each ship holds roughly 1000 passengers and a ratio of at least one crew member for every two passengers (that's a good ratio)
- Crystal is well-known for its world tours – you can start and end in Miami and yet cruise all over the world.

Those are just some of the highlights. You will also experience casual dining options, a really cool cigar room, a casino, cool bars and high attention to detail throughout the ship. Be sure to head up to the Promenade Deck, which is covered in teak. It's absolutely gorgeous. Not to mention upscale boutique type shopping at *Apropos* which includes brands such as Givenchy, Ralph Lauren, Escada, Salvatore Ferragamo, Burberry, Prada, and more.

We were most surprised at the size of the ship. It's pretty big, yet you don't get that big ship feel, as the service and personal attention is incredible.

JUST ADD WATER

Regent Seven Seas (www.rssc.com)

Regent is one of the most well known luxury brands in the cruise industry. You can choose from four ships in their fleet: *Mariner, Voyager* and *Navigator* and, coming soon, *Explorer*. One thing you will really like about Regent Seven Seas is the all-inclusive fares. It makes it easy to plan and budget for your cruise. What's included are airfare, cruise fare, pre- and post-cruise hotel stays, gratuities, shore excursions and beverages including liquor and soda. As a result, while they are a luxury line, you will find they also offer a great value.

Guests onboard will most likely be more professionals and retired couples, who are affluent travelers and who will choose to take 14-plus night voyages.

Their ships are known for being all suite ships. And all but one ship are all-balcony ships (*Navigator* is 90% balconies). And the cabin sizes range from 300 to 2000 square feet. Here are a few more details that we found very cool to the overall, luxury cruise experience outside of what you would expect:

- They give you 15 minutes FREE ship-to-shore phone time for Concierge Suites and above (this is the level we would recommend)
- Their ships are outfitted with European king-size beds—not two twin beds pushed together.

- The staff to guest ratio is 1 to 1.5.
- The only cruise line to offer free unlimited shore excursions in every port-of-call in every destination. You can take as many as you like AND they offer more than one or two choices. For example, in Barbados, they offer eight different options. If you want to dive deeper into a region, they also offer "Regent Choice Shore Excursions" which are a slight supplement.
- You will find various onboard lecturers to add some enrichment to your cruise. Topics range from food, wine, and history specific to the area you are visiting to fine arts, antiques, bridge and more.
- They've recently completed some renovations on *Mariner* and *Voyager* ships, a commitment to keeping their entire fleet fresh.

You will find Regent all over the world. They have cruises in Africa, India, Alaska, Asia/Pacific, Canada/New England, Caribbean, Mediterranean, Northern Europe, South America and Tahiti. Or visit all those places on a Grand Voyage around the world. If you are looking to book a luxury cruise, definitely throw Regent into the mix.

JUST ADD WATER

Silversea (www.silversea.com)

The Silversea fleet includes ships that range from 100 to 540 passengers, three in their expedition line and five in their standard line. Are you seeing a trend here with the luxury lines? Smaller ships, coupled with the ability to get to more intimate and unique locations.

There are a number of distinctions you will find aboard Silversea. Here are a few:

- Intimate, elegant ships – extraordinary space-per-guest ratio;
- Superlative service – nearly one crew member for every guest;
- Butler service for all ships, all guests;
- Open-seating in the restaurant – no assigned time, no assigned table;
- Alternative dining options – multiple venues;
- Gourmet cuisine inspired by Relais & Châteaux; and
- Amazing all-teak decks.

Silversea has options to go to all seven continents in the world. This is pretty unique for a cruise line. Most will hit four or five, but not all seven. Silversea's special expedition ship, *Silver Explorer*, was specifically designed to operate in ice filled waters, such as those in Antarctica and the Arctic. Their itineraries would certainly deliver a very memorable and once-in-a-lifetime experience.

These ships are just the start of the list. There are well over 30 cruise lines around the world. You can explore more on our website.

Pick the Right Ship & Cabin

Now that you have decided on a cruise line, let's go find the right ship! Not all ships within a cruise line are the same. They all offer a variety of "classes," as they call them. The class generally refers to the size and features on the ship. Everything being equal, Kerri and I like to go on the newer ships. They have the latest and greatest things to do, and the most experienced staff.

Choosing the ship is actually pretty easy. If you have decided where and when you want to go, the ship is almost a given. It's different for a Caribbean cruise from Florida, because you have four main ports to choose from (you'll learn more about this in the next chapter), thus giving you different ship options.

JUST ADD WATER

Cabin

Like many first time cruisers, we stayed in an inside cabin. Of course since we had never been on a ship before, we had no idea what the different categories were. The only other time we stayed in an inside cabin, it was a free trip that we had earned for our business. It's just a personal preference.

We always hear "we want the lowest price" or "you don't spend much time in your cabin." Both of those decisions are most likely based on a tight budget, and that's OK. For us, we LOVE hanging out on the balcony with a cup of coffee—or if it's after 9:00 AM, an adult beverage! The one place everyone agrees is THE place to have a balcony is Alaska (where, ironically, because it was a business trip for Kerri, we had an inside cabin). You will enjoy a balcony cabin because on an Alaskan cruise you stay close to the shore. The views are constantly changing. Plus you never know when you might see a whale.

On our honeymoon cruise from Rome, we bought what was at the time called the Penthouse Suite on the *Carnival Dream*. (They have changed the name since. Why, I have no idea.) This place was gorgeous—hardwood floor entry with a writing desk and wine glass cabinet. Spacious living area with a couch, chair and table. Three closets, a dressing area, and a roomy bathroom with not only a toilet, but a floor-mounted drinking fountain next to it! They called it a bidet, which I'm pretty sure is French for "drink here."

The point is, your room shouldn't be an afterthought—the right cabin can make a huge difference in your overall enjoyment of the cruise. So now that you have picked your ship, let's go find you a cabin. Here are the different categories:

Inside - Inside cabins are just what they say. These rooms have no windows, but may have some lighting on the back wall so it looks like there is a window. Especially popular with vampires, there is no way to tell what time of day it is without a watch. One interesting note is that most cabins of any category do NOT have a clock, the way all hotel rooms do.

Ocean View - The only difference between an ocean view and an inside cabin is the window. The square footage is the same. The window can either be a port hole, or a square window. Guess who can help you know which is which?

Balcony - This is the sweet spot. On ANY cruise, we get a balcony whenever we can. Being able to open the door and get some fresh air without having to go to the upper decks is awesome. The size is going to be the same as an inside or ocean view—the only difference is the addition of a balcony, and it's well worth it to pay a few dollars more. We love having a cup of coffee in the morning, and even grabbing a few plates of food from the buffet to enjoy on our private balcony. Want a little more space? Keep reading.

Suites - This is the category that varies widely between both the ships AND cruise lines. There is no "one size fits all" description here as there are with inside, ocean view and balconies. Generally speaking you find much more space, bigger balconies, and more personalized service. Priority boarding is usually one of the perks as well. We have stayed in suites on our wedding, honeymoon and anniversary cruise. If the price isn't prohibitive for you, I always recommend a suite. Suite pries can be a few hundred over a standard balcony to thousands.

Cabin guarantee – A cabin guarantee is just what it says. It guarantees that you have a cabin within whatever category that you book. It's usually the best "lead-in" pricing for most lines. You may not know which cabin you are booked in until time of sailing, but you will generally know much sooner. It allows the cruise line to have flexibility when filling the cabins, and for that flexibility, you get a better price.

Sub-Categories – Nearly all cruise ships have multiple categories within the main cabin types. For example, an oceanview may show five ocean view categories like this: 8A, 8B, 8C, 8D, or 8E. These options reflect sub-categories within a cabin type. The differences are features like a better placement within the ship, mid-ship or higher deck, etc. Be aware the number of categories on each ship vary by cruise ship and cruise line. This can cause a lot of confusion so again, this is where your travel agent can step in and sort it all out for you. Lesson here to learn is not all cabin catories are equal. You will also find the most common price advertised will be a lead in rate. This rate represents the lowest rate in that category.

Which deck to choose? The short answer to that is, it depends on you. The best cabins are usually the highest passenger decks in the middle of the ship. Are you prone to getting sea sick? Then you want a deck and cabin in the middle of the ship. And Dramamine!

If you have stayed in balconies or suites mid ship, you may want to shake it up a bit and get an aft-facing cabin. That is next on our list.

Once you have the ship selected, I recommend getting a deck plan either from your agent or the cruise line website, before you book. See if there is something that you like and want to be close to. For example if you want to be close to the Aqua Show on

JUST ADD WATER

RCI's *Allure* or *Oasis of the Seas*, you need to be at the back of the ship with an inward or an aft facing balcony. Want to be close to the adults-only areas? Find them and choose accordingly. Same goes when wanting a cabin close to the spa (these are generally at the front of the ship).

The Newest Innovations in Cabin Choices

Virtual Porthole Inside Cabin

Thank you, Disney!! In an effort to make inside cabins more attractive, leave it to Disney to come up with a brilliant idea! If you are lucky enough to book an inside cabin on the *Disney Dream*, or *Fantasy*, your cabin will feature a "magic porthole." This porthole is actually a 42" monitor that plays a live feed from cameras on the outside of the ship. These cameras show you what you would see if your room was an ocean view. Basically, it's a big round "window" through which guests can watch the ocean in real time, thanks to a live HD feed. It's incredible that Disney created a demand AND a premium price for a category that was once reserved for price shoppers.

But wait, there's more! You never know when an animated Disney character will "float" by the window. Triggered by sensors when you come in the room, random Disney favorites will pop up on the screen! If you've got kids, they'll truly appreciate this small but fun feature. (OK, I love it too!)

Virtual Balconies - 80" screen

Not to be outdone, industry leader in innovation Royal Caribbean has taken the virtual porthole to a whole new level. Virtual balconies show the cruiser what they would see if they had actually booked a balcony. It debuted on the *Navigator of the Seas* in Feb 2014 in 81 staterooms, and will be featured on every inside stateroom on *Quantum of the Seas* debuting in 2014. One can only assume that this will be a standard Royal Caribbean feature on future ships, like the *Anthem of the Seas* in 2015, as well as the two yet-to-be-named *Oasis* class ships scheduled for delivery in 2016 and 2018.

The high-def views this screen displays are so realistic that they had to add a "virtual railing" because people in a test group said it felt like they could fall in.

Twin Balcony Cabins

In the river cruising category, industry leaders AmaWaterways introduced its unique concept of twin balconies. This has both a French balcony and a small step-out balcony.

CHAPTER FIVE
WHERE CAN I GO?

When Kerri and I started considering locations for our honeymoon in 2009, we both thought of Europe. To us, a honeymoon had to be someplace exotic. Somewhere we had both never been before, and both wanted to experience. No offense to people who want to honeymoon on a warm tropical island, it's just that we live in Florida, and all but one of our cruises at that point had been in the Caribbean. The Mediterranean, and Italy in particular, is incredibly romantic and was always at the top of our dream trips list.

The sheer number of places that you can go on a cruise is overwhelming, even for agents. And that doesn't begin to include the number of cities that are within a short bus ride from the port, which make great shore excursions. There are over 500 ports worldwide, with over 30 in North America alone.

There are cruises designed for everyone, and every type of interest. In some places in Alaska, you can only get there on a cruise. There are adventure expeditions to unique places like Antarctica, the Amazon Rain Forest, or an African safari. Don't want to stray far from the States? Discover history closer to home by exploring New England, French Canada, colonial America, and even America's rivers.

Most people that know us at some point will hear our honeymoon story—a 12-night Mediterranean cruise, round trip from Rome. It was our first trip to Europe. We bought Rosetta Stone, and still only understood a few words (dove il bagno?). We sailed on the *Carnival Dream* from Rome. In this case we picked the destination first and the ship second. After selecting the where, we picked the *Dream* because it was a brand new ship, on its third voyage.

In the coming pages, you will see the majority of ports of call for the big cruise regions. I am not going to list every port available, especially in the regions of North America and Asia. Odds are that if Kerri and I have been to a port, we will give our take on it. If we have not been there personally, we will use expert testimonials. If you happen to work for the Chamber of Commerce for a city that I accidentally left out, my

JUST ADD WATER

apologies, it was not intentional. Please email me at SoSorry@JustAddWaterBook.com.

Here was our itinerary: a 12-night cruise roundtrip from Rome, with one night before in the Eternal City itself, and three nights after in Florence and Tuscany. Here are the details:

Rome – 1 night

Naples

Venice - overnighted here

Dubrovnik

Sicily

Barcelona (missed it)

Monaco (overnighted since we missed Barcelona)

Livorno - Pisa and Florence – 2 nights

Rome – 1 night

So let's explore where you can go and the best itinerary for you. With over 30 cruise lines and 300 plus ships, the choices can be overwhelming. Here's a simple formula to follow.

Why. The first thing to figure out is why are you cruising? If it's a family reunion, you maybe want to pick a ship that has more sea days than port days. The same would be true of a business meeting. A couple on a honeymoon? A port intensive itinerary may be better. If it's just a quick relaxing vacation, a four-to-five day Caribbean cruise is great! Selecting a cruise for a group is very different from picking one for a vacation.

Where. The next step is to choose where you want to go. The where often determines the when. If it's Alaska, you are limited to May through mid September. If Europe, you may want to avoid the winter. If it's the Caribbean, you may want to avoid hurricane season, but otherwise this area is easy to cruise any time of the year.

When. The when is often tied to the where. You may be looking at a summer vacation with the kids, or a holiday cruise, or maybe one tied to a specific event like the British Open.

What. Now you can narrow down the what. This is what ship and what port. When you can answer the above questions, you will immediately be able to narrow down your choices. And if you have a favorite cruise line, the what may be a new ship in their fleet.

JUST ADD WATER

Destinations

We are fortunate to have experienced the three major regions in the cruising world. Alaska, the Caribbean and the Mediterranean, not just as agents, but as customers just like you. It was that love of seeing the world this way that made the decision to be full time agents an easy one.

An entire book can be written on each of the major cruise regions around the world. To break it down so that you can actually go on a cruise instead of spending two years researching them, we will cover the main regions around the world, the most popular destinations, and some "must see" attractions for that area.

For you detail oriented people, you can visit our website , www.AllAboardTV.com, for a more complete list of destinations. We didn't want anyone falling asleep reading this book.

1. Caribbean

In 2014, the Caribbean represented 37.3% of the cruise itineraries and ship deployment as reported by CLIA. Here's what you need to know about this region. The Caribbean cruises are broken up by Western, Eastern and Southern. You can cruise there year round. Most itineraries will sail either Eastern or Western. The only time you will go to both is on a cruise of longer than 7 days. Southern Caribbean routes sometimes include some Eastern or Western ports. Here are the typical cruise ports for each:

Eastern Caribbean: Bahamas (Nassau and Freeport), San Juan, St. Maarten, St. Thomas-US Virgin Islands, St. Kitts, and Tortola-BVI.

Western Caribbean: Key West, Jamaica (Falmouth, Ocho Rios and Montego Bay), Grand Cayman, Cozumel, Honduras (Roatan), Mexico (Costa Maya), and Belize.

Southern Caribbean: St. Lucia, Martinique, Barbados, Antigua, Grenada, Aruba, Curaçao, and Bonaire.

2. Mediterranean

The Mediterranean is the second most popular cruise destination. Like the Caribbean, you can sail the Med year round. However, I would caution you that it will be cooler in the late fall and winter months. This region is also split into Eastern and Western itineraries plus the Greek Isles. If you have never been to Europe, or have dreamed of visiting Italy or Greece, a cruise in this region is a great way to get to know these locations. You will also find some itineraries that include a mix from all over the Med. Here's an overview of some of the key ports in each:

Eastern: Venice, Croatia (Split and Dubrovonik), Corfu, and Bari.

Western: Barcelona, Rome, Cinque Terre, Naples, Sicily (Messina), Livorno (Florence and Pisa), Nice, Provence, Marseille, and Monaco.

Greek Isles: Athens, Mykonos, Santorini, Rhodes, and Ephesus.

3. Alaska

If you plan to take an Alaskan cruise, you will need to plan your vacation between late April and mid-September. You have two main itineraries for Alaska: inside passage and Gulf of Alaska. The one most people think of is the inside passage. So what's the difference?

Inside Passage: Most of these cruises will leave from Vancouver, Seattle or San Francisco. Your itinerary is almost always 7 nights. Ports on this itinerary may include: Juneau, Ketchikan, Sitka, Skagway, and a stop to Glacier National Park.

Gulf of Alaska: If you have more time to explore Alaska, consider this itinerary. The Gulf of Alaska itineraries are a one-way up the coast and can be combined with a land tour. It starts in Anchorage (Seward Port) and ends in Vancouver or Seattle (or the reverse). You will sail to a few of the inside passage ports. The land tours available to add on to your pre- or post-cruise will take you into the heart of Alaska by train. If you are interested in seeing more of Alaska's scenery, you should consider a Gulf of Alaska cruise with land tour.

Expedition Cruises

The first thing I can say about the cruises listed below is they are all on my and Kerri's "Must See List" (we don't have a "bucket" list, that's too depressing for us).

Antarctica

Considered to be one of the last frontiers of cruising, it's on many people's to do list. Of the 21 million who will sail this year, about 20,000 will cruise Antarctica. That's .00095. Want to be the coolest person at a cruise event? Tell them that you have cruised Antarctica. A friend of ours who is one of the best cruise experts we know sailed on Hurtigruten to Antarctica, and she loved it! And, yes, she was the coolest person at the party!

JUST ADD WATER

Galapagos

A very familiar place to anyone that has the Discovery or History channel. Heck, anyone with basic cable or satellite service has probably seen this place. Ask them to find it on a map, and the percentage will drop dramatically. Cruise to "Darwin's Living Laboratory" and you will encounter animals like flightless cormorants, marine iguanas, and domed giant tortoises. National Geographic does great cruises there, and with a name like that….

African Safari

Like many people, we have always dreamed of going on an African Safari. You know, really roughing it, with portable air conditioners and satellite phones. We never even imagined that you could go on a safari while on a cruise. Then again, we didn't even know river cruising existed back then. Even though it's fourth on the list here, it's first on our exotic cruise "to do" list.

We have even picked the trip and itinerary. It's called the "Rivers and Rails of Africa on AmaWaterways" and here are a few details.

"Your African experience begins with a three-night stay in picturesque Cape Town. Next, fly to Kasane to begin your Zambezi Queen wildlife cruise on the Chobe River. Explore the banks of Chobe National Park, home to one of Africa's densest populations of wildlife. Encounter elephants, leopards, lions, gazelles and buffalos on excursions by boat or open-air vehicle. Your journey continues with two nights in Victoria Falls, one of the world's greatest natural wonders. From there, board the Rovos Rail vintage train for a luxurious two-night, 1000-mile journey through Botswana and into South Africa. After your rail journey ends in Pretoria, you will transfer to nearby Johannesburg to relax on your final night in Africa."

Tell me that doesn't sound freakin' amazing!! Love the two nights on the train. And if you want to go with us, let us know!

Amazing World Events

This section is all about dreaming. Traveling to even one of these events is a life changing experience. But why not travel to all of them? Sure it's going take years, but the years are going happen anyway! So get out there and dream big with these incredible events that are even more fun when cruising is the way you get there.

There are a number of great world events you can cruise to, and they change from year to year.

JUST ADD WATER

Here is an example of one incredible event that you probably have heard of, but didn't know you could cruise to.

Monaco Grand Prix

When our honeymoon trip took us to Monaco, it was simply amazing. On one of our excursions, the tour bus drove the course for the Monaco Grand Prix. We even got out of the bus and walked on it to see it better. OK…they DO race on the main streets, but it was awesome none the less. We made a vow, on the spot, to someday return during race week. A race in Monaco has to be a dream trip by anyone's definition. There are many ships in town that week, and to give you an idea, here is the list of the ships that were in Monaco on race day, May 25, 2014.

Azamara Journey

Azamara Quest

Crystal Serenity

Silver Spirit

Star Flyer

Star Pride

Wind Surf

As you may have noticed, these are all premium or luxury ships, but don't worry if you don't have a big budget. Even the

Big lines like Carnival, Norwegian and Royal Caribbean sail here. Just not during this particular time.

The World *Cruise Ship*

Think that cruising even a few months a year is not enough? Don't worry. There's a solution for you. It's called *The World*. No, it's not a joke. That's really the name of the ship! How fun would it be when someone asks you where you live to respond, "the world." What's your address? *The World*! Here it is, in their own words...

"The World is the only private residential community-at-sea where its residents travel the globe without ever leaving home. Since it first set sail in 2002, The World has visited over 900 ports in over 140 countries. With a continuous worldwide itinerary that enables the vessel to span the globe every two-to-three years, the ship is a complete floating city, equipped with high-end facilities and luxurious amenities that create an intimate, refined atmosphere for resident-owners. This strikingly beautiful ship promises gracious and personal service in a warm, inviting ambience much like that of a private yacht, well-staffed private home or exclusive country club.

A lifestyle aboard The World allows residents to explore the planet's most breathtaking destinations with like-minded

JUST ADD WATER

adventure seekers from the comfort of their own private residence. This exclusive community offers the ultimate combination of luxury travel with world-class dining, custom destination experiences, and enriching cultural events like renowned guest speakers, local dancers or art exhibitions. A myriad of exceptional onboard amenities include a gourmet deli, The World Spa & Wellness Center, library, cinema, and a sports center offering real and virtual golf excursions to the world's top-ranked courses. The onboard lifestyle fosters a welcoming atmosphere, a warm sense of community, and encourages the formation of lasting friendships."

Sounds good to me. Start saving now.

CHAPTER SIX
KNOW BEFORE YOU GO

The more you cruise, the more you will learn what to do before you go. Until then, you can learn a few things from our expertise and experience. Here are some things to consider.

Trip Insurance

Like any other insurance, the only time you like trip insurance is when you have to use it. I really don't like car insurance (especially in Florida) or health insurance, but it really is a smart choice. Kerri and I use a third party company as opposed to the cruise line because it's more inclusive. Cruise line insurance covers the cruise, NOT the airfare and other miscellaneous things, like lost luggage. This is so important it warrants another example.

On our wedding cruise, two couples from different cities both had someone who was too sick to travel, and were not able to make it. I know…you may be thinking that was just an excuse to skip the wedding. If it was, it was a very expensive one. Both couples were staying in grand suites for the cruise. They weren't just coming to the wedding, they were cruising with us! They not only lost the cost of the cruise which was about $1200, they also lost money on the airfare! If you are talking with your travel agent, and they forget to bring it up, make sure that YOU do. The right travel insurance would have covered their cruise and travel costs.

Packing

Ah, packing. With the number of "how to pack" videos available and the amount we travel you would think Kerri and I would be master packers. Let's just say you can learn a few tips from our experiences, both good and bad. Like when we first arrived in Italy for our honeymoon and met the driver at the car. The driver said something like "is this all YOUR luggage?" And he didn't mean it in a "did you get everything?" kind of way. Lucky for us he was able to smash everything into the small vehicle. It looked something like a college student packing up their car with all their belongings at the end of the semester. When traveling to Italy, or Europe for that matter, be aware that everything is smaller, from vehicles to sidewalks to hotel rooms and elevators. You'll be grateful you packed light.

It is a natural tendency to over pack. As you lay out your clothes you start talking yourself into more and more "just to be safe." But with the right understanding of where you are going and what you will be doing, you can be a superstar packer. Here are a few packing tips:

1. Flying vs. Driving to the port. Flying to the port? You better have a luggage scale. If you are flying to the port then you need to know that your checked bags can't be over 50 lbs. each without paying extra. This is where having status with an airline is awesome. Kerri and I each can check two bags for free whenever we fly American Airlines. You automatically get two free bags on international flights with most airlines, as well as free drinks during the flight.

2. Luggage. When it comes to luggage, I am a total geek, meaning I love seeing all the different types of luggage that people use. Before I met Kerri I would buy the cheapest luggage at Wal-

Mart, and it would fall apart after a few flights. I really didn't care that much, because I didn't travel that often. After I met Kerri, I not only traveled more, I learned the importance of using quality luggage. I was shocked at the prices she paid for her bags, but soon realized that (like most things) she was right. For years I used a very good brand that I liked and it had a great warranty, then it changed. I now use the only brand in the industry that has three of my favorite words… lifetime, unconditional, warranty. And that is what Briggs and Riley delivers. This is the luggage that Kerri and I use.

Think of luggage pricing as a per use thing. Kerri has a carry-on (say that three times real fast) bag that has been replaced several times so far with a new one. Even the best luggage out there is going to get beat up when traveling, especially when flying. Buying luggage with the best warranty, while still looking good, is our philosophy.

3. What clothes to pack: Of course what you wear depends not only on where you are going, but the time of the year. Bikinis on a Christmas market cruise in Europe? Not unless they have an indoor hot tub. Most ships, whether ocean or river, have a relaxed and casual attitude when it comes to clothing. If it's warm, I'm wearing shorts. If it's chilly, I'm in jeans. Even when filming segments of our show, I'm usually in shorts or jeans.

JUST ADD WATER

Most cruise lines have detailed dress codes on their website. The luxury and premium brands are different than the mass market cruise lines. When in doubt, ask.

Very rare is the trip where I wear everything that I packed. Make a quick plan before you pack. List the days you will be gone, including travel days, and pick the things that you want to wear. As boring as that may sound, it will save you in the long run.

4. *Toiletries*. Most cruise lines provide the basic toiletries in travel size packs such as shampoo, conditioner and lotion. Make sure you bring travel size items that will carry you through the entire vacation. Consider a hanging bag which can easily be put behind doors.

Kerri and I each have toiletry bags that hang, so we don't have to unpack everything in the bathroom—most things can stay in the bag. Eagle Creek has some great items for keeping toiletries organized. Another great idea is to have travel-sized bottles of things you will need most often. Here are the things we keep all the time in our toiletry bag: toothpaste, hair gel, hairspray, contact solution, shampoo and conditioner. Having at least two available is always good. If one container is running low right before a trip, it's easy to grab the full one.

Gadgets and Gear

Who doesn't like gadgets and gear? Here are a few things you probably didn't think about bringing along. Once you're onboard, you'll understand why we recommend packing a few.

Packing Cubes. Gone are the days when I would just throw things in luggage without having a system. Using a system of "packing cubes" has taken the stress out of packing for me. For all of the small stuff, underwear, socks, t-shirts, etc. they each have their own cube. When I am ready to start putting things in the luggage, I just grab the cubes and put them in. And what's even better is when you get on the ship and unpack, you simply pull out the cube and place it in a drawer. Quick and easy. We use Eagle Creek. They come in a bunch of sizes and colors and they are light and won't add much weight. We also have tried the vacuum Space Saver bags. They are ok and your cabin steward will lend you a vacuum on the last day to re-suction your bags.

Power Strip. Yep, a power strip. Your stateroom will most likely have one or two outlets. If you want to charge up more than one or two devices at night, you will need a power strip and they don't offer them onboard. Make this a staple packing item for your cruise.

JUST ADD WATER

Bluetooth Speaker. This is for your in room music (not to be the DJ at the pool). Play some tunes from your iPod/iPhone/Android (whatever you use).

Headphones. Great for when you are hanging out by the pool. Just make sure everyone has their own set.

SmartPhone/Tablet. We list this because it is a common question.

INSIDER TIP: Put your devices in airplane mode. Most people use their smartphone as their main camera. Make sure you have plenty of room on your device before you go. A tablet can be great for reading a book, or for many, playing candy crush by the pool. We see this EVERY cruise. It's probably more popular than bingo.

A Day Bag and Ziplocs. Pack a light bag you can use for your shore excursions and throw in some Ziploc bags. If you hit a beach, put your phone in the Ziploc to keep it sand free. You can also use your day bag as your carry-on bag since your actual luggage may take a few hours to arrive at your cabin.

Walkie Talkies. Great way to stay connected with your party while on the ship. This is getting to be slightly old technology.

Many of the newer ships have apps you can text others in your party through your smartphone free of charge. Or, if you are on Disney, the rooms come with Walkie Talkies. Be sure to check what your ship does or doesn't offer before you go.

An "over the door" shoe organizer. Perfect for longer cruises if you are in a smaller stateroom. This is a clever item to pack and use for something other than shoes. You can put a variety of items in the pockets from bathroom products to a place to keep your carry around items like travel mugs, lanyard, medicine, and poker chips.

Tie rack for jewelry. A great item to use for hanging your necklaces and other accessories. That way, they don't get all mixed up and tangled like they do when you just place them in a drawer or on a counter.

Magnets/Magnetic hooks. Your stateroom door and some walls in your cabin are metal. Use magnets to post things on your wall like the daily program or notes for your cabin steward. Or you can bring along some magnetic hooks for an additional place to hang a towel, jacket or handbag.

Alcohol

It's good to know what you can and can't do in regard to alcohol onboard before you go. So grab a drink and read on. (PS. You may need to read this section twice; we had a few while we wrote it).

The first thing that most people see when they board a cruise is the friendly waiter or waitress with a fruity tropical drink with a mini umbrella. Before you reach out for that drink, you better have your sign and sail card. I see it on almost every cruise—people who reach for the drink thinking it's "on the house." It's not, on most cruises.

What is or is not allowed when it comes to adult beverages varies so much, that I will cover general info, and is yet another reason to work with a cruise travel agent.

What You Can Bring Onboard

Most cruise lines allow you to bring on one bottle of wine or champagne per adult. Some will charge you a corkage fee if you bring it to the restaurant. You pay nothing if you consume it in your stateroom. Be aware however some cruise lines will make you pay a corkage fee for each bottle before you even get on the ship. Not a big fan of that. Seriously, if a couple goes out of their way to bring two bottles of wine with them, is that all they are going to drink on a seven day cruise? Not Likely.

Of all the cruise lines, Disney is the best when it comes to bringing your own booze. Instead of one bottle per person, how about one carry on per person...SOLD! If you drink wine or liquor, one carry on per person can save you hundreds of dollars, and can make up a good chunk of the price difference between Disney and other large lines. Now, Disney gets the highest prices as far as large cruise ships go, but they are the most brilliant marketers EVER! And talk about clean ships. Rarely will you see a Disney ship in port that is not being hosed down by multiple workers.

Drink Packages.
Just about every cruise line that is not all-inclusive offers some type of drink package. It started with soda packages, and then the parents said "hey, what about us?" The big cruise lines rolled this out to such success that it's now common on most of the cruise lines. These packages however vary GREATLY depending on the line you are sailing on. Keep this in mind. Most packages require both adults in the cabin to pay, and the package must be purchased for every day that you are on the cruise. I know some of you people are already thinking...I'll just buy the package on the sea days. On the days we are in port, I won't need it. Nice try

JUST ADD WATER

Sherlock. The cruise lines are WAY ahead of you. That's how they can afford to let you drink plenty of drinks on sea days. They know you won't drink as many on port days – duh, you're not on the ship, it's the law of averages. Caution: many people will get the drink package, be in full on vacation mode and go on a two day binge, drinking everything in sight, and spend the rest of the cruise hung over. Don't do that. Pace yourself. Trust me. I have had some sea days turn into "recovery" days.

For those of you that are not professional drinkers, here is a good rule of thumb. Take the price of the package per day. Don't forget to add in tax AND gratuity…I know, I know. Now factor in the drinks you will have most often. If you are a beer drinker, don't think you are going to jump to hard liquor, and drink the same number of drinks. I'm a beer drinker, and most beers are $5 - $6 onboard. If the package is $49.95 and you add in tax and tip the $49.95 per day package is now about $60. Divide that by the price of a beer, and I need to drink 10 beers a day to break even. No problem…but don't forget the days you are in port and buying drinks on land. If you drink just a couple beers a day, the drink package wouldn't be a good deal. You with me?

For a comparison, save ALL of your drink receipts in an envelope, whether you get a drink package or not. Add up the total and see if it's higher or lower than the drink package. That's great info for your next cruise. I know some people that did not take that advice, and ended up spending more to get off the ship than they did to get on. Meaning their bar tab was more than their cruise fare. Well done!

I recently heard that one line was considering limiting the number of drinks per day. From a customer perspective, that just pisses me off. If a drink package has limits, then it's not really a drink package at all. It's more like a discount for bulk buying; Sam's Club at sea. In the same way, a happy hour bucket of beer for $12 at your local bar is not a drink package.

Update: As I was putting the finishing touches on this book, cruisers took to the internet going nuts over drink package changes on some cruise lines. As we looked into it, we found that Norwegian Cruise Lines had made some changes. I will copy the change to the drink policy here:

"This package is not available for purchase on charters, sailings that are four (4) days or less and Pride of America. Also not available during blackout dates of March 1 – April 15…"

Let me interpret. "Sailings of 4 days or less" is because of people turning these into "booze cruises," mostly from Florida ports. I have seen it happen where on these short 3-4 day cruises,

JUST ADD WATER

people get "zombie/blackout" drunk. I get why the cruise lines are doing it. Drink packages are relatively new, and like most things, the passengers quickly find a way to take it to the extreme. It affects the safety of their passengers and also the bottom-line for the cruise line.

As far as charters go, they are referring to cruises done in partnership with Sixthman. Their expertise is full-ship charters for music groups and their fans. No surprise here that fans of certain rock groups are known to drink in huge amounts. Think of it this way—if a hard-partying band, say KISS, was doing a four day land party, and everybody could drink as much as they wanted for $50 per day, the place would lose money.

The obvious dates to note are no drink packages during March 1 - April 15th. Spring Break. Tell a college student they can drink all they want for $50 per day on a cruise, and that will not only sell out fast, they will run out of booze! With the number of people going on spring break cruises that are under 21, there is almost no way to police the underage drinking, and the "jails" on the ship can only handle a few people at a time. Additionally, there are families aboard who really aren't going to be interested in a future short spring break cruise if everyone on the ship is "overdoing" the bar.

If you think about it, it's just math. I know people that can easily go on a three to four day "bender." Try five days or more, and you need a day or two to recover. It's hard to drink huge amounts of alcohol for five to seven days straight, but for many people, three to four is no problem. If someone buys the drink package on a seven-night cruise, the cruise lines know that they will drink substantially less on at least two-to-three of those days—either because they were recovering, or because they were off the ship on port days.

All three of the above references are just another example of the few f******…I mean, screwing it up for the many! It happens in life, and it happens in cruising. It's easy to blame the cruise lines, but their number one goal really is the safety of their passengers. You think it's bad when they lose power for awhile? Think about what would happen if they had to keep stopping to look overboard for drunk-ass people that can't hold their liquor.

Passport

Passports have been a hot, although boring topic, for the past few years. Here's my opinion: just get one. If I had a dollar for every person that asked me that question, I could pay for a

JUST ADD WATER

cruise with it. They are cheap, and add a lot to your cool factor. Technically you don't need one to get on or off a ship, in MOST ports leaving from the US. Here is why you should get one anyway. If for whatever reason you can't get back on the ship when out of the U.S., illness, or too many drinks at Carlos and Charlie's, you can't fly back to the States without one.

Photos/Video

High on your packing list should be a camera and video camera. Basic, right? Yet many people get off their cruise and kick themselves for not getting some photos of their favorite parts of the cruise. Here are some tips.

One of the best things you can do is plan your shot list in advance. Take a few minutes and write down a few "must have" photos. Things like getting a shot of your cabin BEFORE you unpack and mess it up. Or getting a photo with your wait staff and *maître d'* that waited on you with great service. Taking photos with you and the new friends you met so you can send them a card after the cruise. Or even making sure your entire family gets more than just one photo of everyone together, especially when you have a group or multi-generational group cruising together.

The ship will most likely have photographers onboard as well. They take great staged photos. They are not following you around to capture every moment, that's up to you. You can expect onboard photographers to be around for an embarkation photo, before/after dinner photos each night, during dinner (yeah, we never get this one), and when you get off the ship in ports of call.

Most cruise lines will print the photos they take and have them in an area you can view them. They even have a storage area so you can set aside the photos you like each day and then at the end of the cruise buy them together.

The photo packages come in as many shapes and sizes as there are cruise lines and cruise ships, and some even make the digital versions available. Don't be shy about getting your photos taken. They may catch a unique perspective on the ship you had not yet thought of, but one that they see week after week.

When we got married, part of the package was using the ship's photographer. I admit I was a little nervous. The wedding photographer is one of the most important people. But what I quickly discovered upon reviewing our photos was that the onboard photography team knows all the really cool and unique spots and angles on the ship to capture you in not only great light, but also some spectacular backdrops.

JUST ADD WATER

And yes, there are still those cheesy, old school type photos. Some people like those I guess. But go up to the top decks on formal night and you will probably see a photographer up there capturing shots of people all dressed up while the sun is setting behind them. AND they have the lighting to make sure your face is seen, and not just a silhouette.

INSIDER TIP: If you wait until that last day of your cruise to select and finalize the photos you want to purchase from the ship, you will find yourself in a HUGE line, and will probably get quite frustrated trying to make so many photo decisions (especially if your cruise was seven days or more). As a result, you will end up spending more money than you need to because you will concede and say "buy them all." Instead, either purchase photos throughout the cruise, or have the photos set aside by the staff so you don't have to make decisions that last day when it can get busy.

ROB & KERRI STUART

CHAPTER SEVEN

LIFE ONBOARD

L ife Onboard is an experience that never gets old. So what exactly do you do? We are going to cover the basics: Food, Activities and Entertainment, and some of the Logistics of life onboard (they aren't that exciting so we put them at the end of this chapter).

Food

It is always surprising to hear about a novice cruiser who wasn't aware there were more dining options than the popular buffet, and missed out on the dining room experience. Don't let this be you. Cruises are well known for offering some of the best cuisine. And the options are plentiful. And don't worry, it is possible to eat sensibly and not gain 15 pounds on your cruise. There are so many different dining choices among the ships that I will put this in general terms.

The Buffet

The buffet is the most popular option. You'll find it on one of the top decks and close to the pool area. You can build up your plate and head out to the deck or stay inside. Most likely, the buffet will be the place you first eat when you board the ship. The buffets offer nearly unlimited food choices for breakfast, lunch, dinner and snacks. You will find a huge variety of food choices such as salad fixings, fresh soups, sandwiches, pasta dishes, Chinese dishes, steak, chicken, pork, grilled veggies, hamburgers, hot dogs, Indian dishes, cheese platters, fresh fruit, nacho bar, and so on.

Main Dining

Most cruise lines assign you a main dining room for dinner. When you book your cruise you request early or late dining. Early is usually 6 and late 8:30. Thanks to Norwegian and the "Freestyle Dining" concept, most cruise lines have added an "anytime" dining as an option. It's just that, go eat when you want.

I enjoy eating in the main dining room most nights. Especially because the wait staff is the same and they know to have my beer and Kerri's wine ready when we arrive. You will quickly fall in love with having a wait staff tend to your every need at dinner. Most of all, I enjoy getting to meet other passengers we are seated with and hearing about their day and getting to know them.

The main dining rooms don't just serve dinner but also breakfast and lunch. The menu will be limited. And most of all we find it is much more quiet and relaxing compared to the buffet.

Speciality Restaurants

Specialty restaurants are all the rage and VERY much worth the $25 - $30 per person cover charge. Not too say that eating with a few hundred of your closest friends isn't fun, but for a nice romantic dinner for two, the specialty restaurants will be a better option. There are also more casual specialty restaurants being added like a cupcake/sweets shop, pizza, hamburgers, etc. Just check the list of restaurants on your ship. And if you are a foodie, we highly recommend you check into a "Chef's Table" at least once. This is available on several of the larger ships and is usually limited to just 12 people per cruise. It's pricy, but well worth it. Be sure to book specialty restaurants early (or better yet before your cruise), as they can fill up pretty fast.

Snacks

All around the ship you will find different snacks. If you ever go hungry on a ship, it's your own fault. Some of the popular snacks will be the ice cream machine (if you can battle around the kids to get to it), the midnight specialty buffets they put out, and the 24 hour pizza buffets. You get the idea. If you are looking for a snack, you can find it.

Room Service

Most cruise lines offer free room service for the nights or mornings when you are too hung over, I mean tired, to venture out of the cabin. A midnight BLT and chips with a bowl of soup is our standard order. At least once on a cruise, Kerri and I will order it whether we are hungry or not just because it is fun to sit on the balcony and enjoy a nice view and a meal delivered to our room.

Activities & Entertainment

There is so much to do on a cruise. There is literally something for everyone and every age. Here are some of the most popular things to do on a cruise. You will find these on most cruise ships and you may even discover some we left off this list.

JUST ADD WATER

Pools and the Deck - Adult and Kids

The pools on a cruise ship are the most popular activity, especially for the Caribbean and Mediterranean cruises. And with many people taking vacations in the cooler months and coming from states where the sun has been hiding all season, people want to just sit and enjoy the sun. The pools on ships are great. You will quickly see rows and rows of lounge chairs and people of all ages in the pool. Scout out the different pools and see which is the best for you, or find the right place to park yourself and enjoy the sun.

Most ships have a main pool. If your idea of a cruise is a lot of kids running and jumping in the pool, entertainment around the pool, or pool games, then the main pool is a good place for you. It is a fun area and GREAT people watching if you're into that.

But don't worry. If you are looking for a little more quiet and relaxed pool, most ships have an adult only area. The larger the ship, the more pools they usually have. It helps spread the people over a larger area so it doesn't feel so crowded. If you walk around on the first day, you will quickly find the right pool for you. And if you want to just be in a quiet place on the deck reading a book, you can usually go up a deck higher than the main pool and find a lounge chair.

Hot tubs are another big draw. When we were in Alaska, we were surprised to find we were the ONLY ones in the hot tub ever. It was quite chilly outside. The hot tubs are a great place to relax and they will be spread out. You may even find a hidden one on some ships where very few people hang out.

Water Parks

Even at our age, Kerri and I love water parks. With each cruise line trying to outdo the other, water parks and water slides are becoming more and more creative. Here are the lines that shine when it comes to having fun while getting wet: Carnival, Disney, Royal Caribbean, Norwegian and MSC. A really cool slide is the "trap door" slide where you stand vertically and the floor below you drops out and you fall into the water slide tube. Fun and scary. Disney even built an elevated lazy river where you sit on an innertube and go through a clear tube that sits above the deck. Pretty cool, but don't expect lightening fast speeds.

Spa

The spa is often a first stop for experienced cruisers on embarkation day. Often you will find "Sail Away" deals with better pricing. A great time to book spa appointments is on a port day as they offer the best deals then to keep you onboard (if you are not onboard, you are not spending money with them). You can also buy a day or week pass to access select areas of the

JUST ADD WATER

spa like the sauna, thermal pool, and relaxation rooms anytime you choose.

Sports Facilities

A staple on many larger ships, basketball at sea is very popular, with some courts even converting to small soccer fields complete with spectator stands. Some have tennis courts as well. There is netting all around so no need to worry about losing the ball overboard during your game. The courts will primarily be on the most upper deck either near the front or the back of the ship.

Mini Golf

Always a lot of fun. Add a few adult beverages, and it gets even more fun! Want to take it to the next level? How about the winner gets the spa treatment of their choice!

Adventure Activities

Adventure has become something new and you will find them primarily on the newer ships. Adventure activities are things like a FlowRider® (a kind of simulated surfing), ice skating, rock wall climbing, zip line, rappelling, ropes course, trampoline, 4D theaters, Formula One racing, etc. Just keep in mind these activities will have very set times, may get quite busy and may have some restrictions or require a fee. They are pretty cool and something different if you aren't into water-based activities.

Bingo

I am amazed at the number of people who play bingo like it's a profession. If bingo is offered on the ship, you can bet it will be packed! There will be multiple bingo opportunities throughout your cruise.

Port Talks

Still haven't decided what you want to do in port? Each day the cruise staff will talk about things to do at your next port of call. It's usually done in the main theater, but if you miss it, you can catch it on one of the shipboard TV channels. It is also a great way to learn about the different shopping opportunities in the next port as well. The presenters are extremely informed and can answer questions. They will also provide you with a map of the port and some key places to shop. They may even have a couple of coupons.

Art Auctions

This has been a hot topic over the last few years. On almost every cruise, I have seen art auctions. I have never bought any piece of art either on or off the ship, so this is really not my thing. I do however see many people attending these, some just for the

JUST ADD WATER

free champagne. Park West is the big player here and works with these cruise lines, according to their website: Carnival, Celebrity, Holland America, Norwegian, Regent and Royal Caribbean. As with most things, let the buyer beware. Don't think that you will stumble on a priceless masterpiece after spending a few hours at the pool bar. If you like what they are selling, and it's in your budget, by all means have at it.

The Gym

Kerri and I always bring our workout shoes, and have yet to ever exercise on a ship (well, maybe we did once). Of course that could be a carry-over from not working out at a gym on land either, but we always fool ourselves into thinking we will hit the gym at sea. We do go at least look at it. You should too. If you are into exercise, you will find many options to keep you busy and sweating onboard. They also offer things like yoga sessions, spin classes, or Zumba where you pay a small fee. *MSC Divina* even offers a water spin class (yes, bikes in the pool). There are no charge options as well. The gyms are generally packed with equipment from free weights, weight machines, treadmills, stationary bikes, elliptical trainers, kettle bells and really most of what's popular in exercise at the moment. Or you can walk or run on the track up on deck. Norweigian's new ships even have an outdoor circuit training.

Kids Programs at Sea

The obvious top factor in family vacations is the kids. Will they have enough to keep them busy and have fun? Parents, relax. Cruises do this better than any other vacation option, including theme parks. All of the major cruise lines have kids programs broken down into different age groups for kids from three to 17 that are free. If you do have a child under three, there are some "programs" but we will just call it babysitting. You do pay an hourly or day rate. And if you do have an infant, no cruise lines will allow you to bring on a baby less than six months old at the time of sailing. Disney used to allow kids as young as three months but changed that policy in 2014. Most cruise lines break up kids into the following age brackets: 3-5, 6-8, 9-11, 12-14, and 15-17.

Kids are suckers of characters and name brands. The cruise lines know this and have affiliations with some pretty big names. Sometimes this alone is a reason your kids will like a certain cruise line. Most activities are free, but there are a few that you will need to reserve and pay for. Not all the ships in each class will have the brand name programs so ask your agent so your little one isn't disappointed when he/she gets on the ship expecting a specific character to be there like they saw in a brochure. Here are a few of those, along with any affiliation they have to a major entertainment brand.

- *Dreamworks Experience* – Royal Caribbean, *Allure, Oasis, Freedom, Liberty* and *Quantum*.
- *Nickleodeon* - Norwegian - five ships. *Gem, Jewel, Epic, Breakaway,* and *Getaway*.
- *Barbie® Premium Experience* – Royal Caribbean, all ships.
- *The Smurfs* – MSC, *Divina*.
- *Mickey Mouse, Princesses and other Disney Characters* – Disney Cruise Lines, entire fleet

Specialty Classes, Tastings & Enrichment Classes

Crystal and Seabourn are the leaders in offering enrichment classes at sea. These generally include a lecture led by an expert in their field. It can range from a history lesson to a computer class. Celebrity even has a GoPro program for kids to shoot and edit their own vacation video.

If you like to learn about drinks, you will find classes for beer, wine, cocktails, champagne and whiskey. We've gone to the trouble of personally testing all these out for you, and can assure you they are very informative.

Arcade

The arcade is like a kid's casino. They can load up a card with money and then play to their heart's content. Or until they run out of money. Most arcades are small and carry a mix of the new and old games, things like Pac Man and Street Fighter to new games like Dance Dance Revolution. The arcade isn't free. Check with the ship to see how you can limit the amount the kids can charge to the room.

Library

I have no idea how this made the list, but what the hell. Many people bring a good paperback to read on the cruise, but the new trend is eBook readers like iPad and Kindle. Your cruise ship will have a library as well, in case you forgot your book or just want to say you checked out a library book on a cruise ship.

Duty Free Shopping

Yes, there is shopping on a cruise ship. And it isn't just the souvenirs and sundries type shopping, we're talking REAL shopping. Designer clothes and handbags (Kerri's favorite), and high end watches (my favorite) are at the top of the list. If you are into these items, check pricing at a regular retailer and then when onboard you can know if you are getting a great deal. You will also find name brand cosmetics, fragrances, costume jewelry and watches. Again, this is a good deal if it is something you were already going to purchase anyway. There will be crazy sales like the $10 sale that had a line going down the hall. Or a 40% off watch sale. One of the big reasons shopping is popular on cruise ships is because it is duty free. So, if you've been thinking of getting high-end items like, say, a new Tag Heuer watch, you will be saving some cash from the taxes, as well.

And if you do have a problem with something you purchase, they have a 100% satisfaction guarantee so you can certainly get any item replaced by their service center if something happens. They also have a "best price" guarantee. They are keenly aware they are competing with shops in port. It is important to note that the stores on the ship are rarely open when in port. So plan your shopping on sea days or during the evening. And be sure to keep an eye out for some great sales.

They also sell liquor, wine and tobacco at great prices. Keep in mind when you purchase these items, you won't receive them right then. Instead, the ship will set aside and deliver the purchase to your stateroom on the last night of the cruise.

Shows: Main Theater

As the ships get bigger and bigger, so does the entertainment. From Broadway productions and ice shows to water shows, the cruise lines are constantly trying to one-up each other, to the passengers delight.

Specialty Shows

As new ships come out, the various cruise lines have really challenged each other to reinvent and provide unique entertainment. No longer are "variety shows" the norm. Now, you have everything from water shows to cirque-type shows to rock concerts. Here are some of the options you can find on a cruise ship.

Ice Shows / Water Shows

Since Royal Caribbean has cornered the market on ice rinks at sea, it makes sense that they are the only ones with ice shows. Kerri and I have seen the ice rink on *Allure of the Seas*. It is pretty cool and a fun indoor activity during your day but then also some fun evening entertainment to watch some fancy skating.

Another head nod to Royal are their water shows located in the Aqua theaters at the aft portion of both *Oasis of the Seas* and *Allure of the Seas*. This show involves divers, acrobats, some fancy choreography and a high tech pool with a floor than can raise and lower. In certain cabins you can see the show from your balcony.

JUST ADD WATER

Cirque-Style Shows

There are a couple of cruise lines that have incorporated cirque-style shows on their ships. You may have seen a Cirque du Soleil show in Vegas. The audience watches as a unique storytelling experience unfolds, supported by performers/athletes with amazing talents. It's something unique to experience. And it's even more impressive when you realize they are doing crazy acts all on a moving ship. Royal Caribbean, Norwegian and MSC all offer some of these types of shows on select ships. A few ships have also added some cirque type performers in the main atrium area.

Movies at Sea

As technology has improved, so has the ability to have a giant screen outdoors that is bright enough to project a sharp image. We started seeing more and more ships upgrade their outdoor deck to include a giant screen in the last five years. During the day they will show movies, clips from onboard shows or activities or just general information. In the evening, the screen often is a place to go and watch a blockbuster movie. In addition to the outdoor movies, several ships will show movies in theaters on the ship. Sometimes they are specifically designed to be movie theaters and other times they are the main theater that just has a large screen. If you don't get the chance to watch movies when you are busy working, it is fun to take some relaxed time on the ship and catch up. You can also get movies in your room as well.

Broadway Shows

Cruise lines bring on Broadway-caliber shows. When you think about how much it costs to see some of these shows in New York, or even when they visit your city, this only adds to the great value a cruise offers.

Here are a few of the standout shows worth mentioning

Rock of Ages – Breakaway, Norweigian Cruise Lines. This show is awesome. Kerri and I saw this on Broadway, and Norwegian does it very well on the *Breakaway*. I am an 80's guy. I loved the decade, and still listen to the music. You will hear songs from Journey, Foreigner, Poison, Europe, REO Speedwagon, and more. I love the music and Kerri says it's a cute story. Either way you will enjoy it.

Blueman Group – Epic, Norwegian Cruise Lines. This is another show that Kerri and I both loved. Although there is absolutely no talking in the show, it's definitely not quiet. Even though the franchise has been around since 1987, this is still a can't miss show on *Epic,* even if you have seen them before in other places like Vegas or Orlando.

JUST ADD WATER

Richard III – Cunard, Queen Mary 2 – This is traditional theater performed by graduates of the prestigious Royal Academy of Dramatic Art. They do one-hour versions of classics, currently including some Shakespeare.

Michael Jackson Tribute – Divina, MSC – the lead entertainer does an amazing dance tribute to Michael Jackson. We enjoyed this show a lot. We knew the songs, the performance was amazing and the other passengers agreed. I think there were two standing ovations.

Other broadway style shows you can find include:

- *Legally Blonde – Getaway*, Norwegian Cruise Line
- *Burn the Floor - Breakaway* and *Getaway*, Norwegian Cruise Line
- *Hairspray – Oasis of the Seas*, Royal Caribbean
- *Chicago – Allure of the Seas*, Royal Caribbean.

Comedy

I love comedy, and watching comedians on a ship while having a few drinks is a blast. Carnival really set the bar high with their partnership with George Lopez, but there are plenty of good comedy shows on other lines as well. You can always find some solid comedians on each ship. They perform only on select nights. The ships also rotate comedians so you may not get the same experience even if you sailed on the same ship and came back a year later. Most have a family friendly show and a late night adult show. Don't bring the kids to that one.

Magic Acts

We both are big fans of magic, and by far the best magician at sea is Chip Romero. We met him as he was performing on a New Year's Eve cruise on the Norwegian *Epic*. He is famous for having sailed over 850 weeks. That's 5,950 days! Do the math. Divide 850 weeks by 52 and that's over 16 YEARS at sea. Chip often gets off one ship and goes right to another. *And* he gets paid for it. What a gig! He is a true ambassador to everything magic. We not only got to meet him, but his dad happened to be onboard as well. It was quite a treat for us to have dinner with the two of them at the Cirque show that night.

Piano Bars

If you like pianos, you're in luck. Whether it's a late night piano bar with a glass of good wine, or tossing back a few beers at dueling piano bars like "Howl at the Moon," it's always a good time. Just remember that the dueling piano bars can get a little racy after 10:00 PM or so. Want to hear your favorite song? Tip the players. The bigger the tip, the faster they play your song. Cash only—no slots for the sign-and-sail card on the piano!

JUST ADD WATER

Casinos

Here is my five cents (adjusted for inflation). If you can't afford to lose the money, stay away from the casinos. They are not there for your entertainment, contrary to what you may think. Just like Vegas, they are there to make money. If the thought of losing $5 or $10 makes you a little light headed, you would be better served by avoiding them at all costs, pun intended.

Casinos are only open when the ship is in international waters. Don't expect them to be open in port, or even as the ship is just leaving. They know exactly the minute the ships hit that mark so they can turn on the machines. If they could have them on in port, they would. Casinos are one of the main ways they make a ton of money, and are able to keep the cruise fares relatively low.

INSIDER TIP: Make sure you get the "players card" for the cruise line. It's a different card from your room key, and will use points to track how much you play. The rewards vary from cruise line to cruise line, and embarkation day is a great time to learn what those rewards are. And if you do spend a lot of time in casino, be sure to learn about some of the perks once you've met certain playing thresholds ($$ spent). You can sometimes receive complimentary drinks or even a free cruise.

Slots and Video Poker

If you like playing these types of games, just make sure that you are using your Players Card to track your play. On ships that do have slot machines, you can expect to find multiple tournaments during the cruise. Each ship will have their own selection of video games.

Table Games

Most of the games we list in this book have a $5 minimum bet, and a $200 maximum bet. On the blackjack or craps tables, you can skirt that maximum by making multiple bets. If you don't know what that means, stick to the other games.

Blackjack: Like at most casinos, blackjack is very popular. There most likely will be variations of the game onboard to choose from, and some you can even see the dealer's hole cards. Check with your casino host to find out when and if they have blackjack tournaments.

Craps: If you want to find the craps table, just listen for all of the people yelling. There are usually only one or two tables on any of the ships at most, and they fill up fast, because they are not full-sized tables. If you have never played, you may just want to watch and have a drink. Don't get sucked in by watching someone who wins thousands of dollars. You weren't there to see how much they may have been down at that point. You may watch them win thousands not realizing they had already been down by five to six thousand, and were just making a strong comeback.

Other Games: This includes things like baccarat, roulette, and a variety of poker games. Again, each ship will vary, and a great time to check out what's available is after you board the ship and want to explore. That's also a great time to introduce yourself to the casino host. Even if you are not betting big, knowing the host can have some advantages!

Poker: Want to really combine poker and cruising? You can't go wrong with the World Poker Tour Cruise - WPTCruise.com.

In a past life, I had a poker business with Kevin Harrington from *Shark Tank*, and actresses Jenny McCarthy and Shannon Elizabeth. I had the opportunity to meet the hosts of the WPT, Mike Sexton, and Vince Van Patten. They are a blast to hang out with, and if you love poker and cruising, you will love this event!

Even though poker is not as big as it once was, you still see Texas Hold 'Em on many larger ships. A few cruise lines have live dealers. The challenge with that is how slow the game moves, especially for people who either don't play much, or who have never played at all. My favorite is the Poker Pro table. This table is the size of a regular poker table with a large video screen in the middle and a smaller screen at each player position so you can see your own cards and make your bets. It definitely keeps the game moving at a face pace. Nothing can throw off someone's momentum more than waiting for a slow player to count their chips to make the right bet. The Poker Pro table is also a lot easier for beginniners since it's very easy to learn. Like any other casino game, if have you any questions just ask the casino host for help.

The People You Meet

And we can't forget to talk about one of the best things ever about cruising, and that's the really cool people you meet from all over the world. And not just the guests onboard—we have met some awesome people who live and work on the ship, as well. To this day we stay in touch with people that we cruised with years ago.

On one occasion, Kerri and I were dressed up for formal night. I was in a white dinner jacket with a red bow tie, and she was in a gorgeous red dress. As we stepped out of the elevator to go to dinner, Kerri was holding our Nikon camera that we use to film our show. A very nicely dressed man saw us and said, "Whoa…can I take a picture of you?" Yes, Kerri looked THAT hot. We said, "of course, that would be great. Also, if you could have your friend take a picture of the three of us together, just so people will believe that all of this happened." He laughed and said "sure, let's do it." The man…Alex Trebek! This was just one of the great stories from the Turner Classic Movies Cruise… more on that in the chapter on groups.

Everyone has an email address these days, and with the popularity of social media sites like Facebook, Twitter and Instagram, social sharing has become a phenomenon. It's also become a way for people that love to cruise to stay in touch. It's my opinion you will meet people who will become lifelong friends, and you may even end up taking a cruise with these new friends.

Logistics

The following logistics are good to know, especially if you are new to cruising. This topic may not be super entertaining, but we promise you'll learn a little something.

Checking In

If you have ever checked in at the airport for a flight, then the check-in process for a cruise ship won't be too foreign. If you haven't, don't worry. It's easy. Check in is slightly different for ocean cruises versus river cruises and, for this chapter, we are going to focus on the ocean-going cruise ships. Because you will be going into international waters and visiting countries outside the US, there is a little more involvement in checking passengers in and making sure they have all the proper documentation. So your check-in actually begins online before you get to port. We recommend you do this before your cruise but you can start the process months before. Online check-in will include entering your passport information, emergency contact information and how you will be paying for onboard expenses. It is highly recommended you complete this because it will speed up your entry to the ship immensely.

Embarkation (Getting on the Ship).

Most ocean cruises board four to five hours prior to sailing. The cut-off of getting on the ship is generally 90 minutes - two hours before the ship is scheduled to leave the port (always check for your specific cruise). We highly recommend you get to the port earlier than a couple of hours before your cruise so you can board the ship and enjoy your afternoon onboard.

JUST ADD WATER

A few thousand people just got off the ship two to three hours before you walked on. So the cabin steward is most likely still getting your cabin ready. This is the time to explore the ship, have a drink, and grab a bite to eat. I always recommend having a carry-on bag with you. Make sure you have sunscreen and swim suit if you want to hang out at the pool. Also have your camera handy. You're probably smiling from ear to ear, and it's a great time to grab that picture for Facebook or Instagram!

Cashless Society

When you check in at the port you are issued a card. It is often called a "sign and sail" card. The newest ships have just introduced a "smart" wristband which has a chip in it and serves the same purpose, but that's only on one ship at the time of writing this book. This card (or wristband) not only opens the door to your room, it tracks when you get on and off the ship, and it's also how you pay for everything on the ship—drinks, bingo, gift shop items, etc. Your card also identifies your dining time and dining location for evening meals (if applicable) and your muster station. The exception here is in the casino, and that depends on the game you are playing. Some require you to use a debit card to get cash to gamble with. Bring or buy a lanyard to keep your card handy at all times. You will be using it a lot. The front desk or the casino will also punch a hole in it for you if you want to add to a lanyard.

Daily Planner

Different cruise lines call them different things, but it's basically a daily newsletter of everything to see and do on the ship on a daily basis. A printed version is delivered to your stateroom by your cabin steward, or you can pick one up at the guest services desk on most ships. On some ships, you can find it on a TV channel or their app as well.

INSIDER TIP: Read the daily program, and carry it with you all the time. It will become a key part of being in the know of what is happening on the ship each day.

Gratuities

A gratuity is always tied to good service. In the US, it is very common to tip your waiter 15-20% of the total bill price based on their service, or, at a bar, a dollar a drink.

Tipping on a cruise ship is different than what one may expect. You will be charged a per-person/per-day rate and it will appear on your final bill. Luxury ships and river cruises have different policies and sometimes include any tipping into the cruise fare, so you think there is no gratuity being added. And sometimes you can get a special that includes all your gratuities. This can be a special the cruise lines run called "Free Pre-Paid Gratuities," or if you are bringing on a group, they may include all gratuities in your overall group price. So, if you have been on a cruise and have never seen this line item, just know that somewhere along the way it was paid for, by someone. So, in reality, it is more of a service charge in my opinion, but a valid one.

It is important to understand that the gratuities charged on a cruise ship are what are used to pay the service staff their wage. It actually makes up a good portion of their compensation. And remember, the fee is for each person in the cabin. Even the little ones; after all, they are still eating, having their beds made, etc.

In recent years, the cruise lines began automatically adding the tip to the statement. One of the big reasons was that the number of international passengers coming on US cruises was rising. And if you've been to Europe, you know that they are not used to tipping. The other reason is that, with the increase in the number of specialty dining options, no longer do you have the exact same waiters every evening. As a result, it became easier to establish a base daily rate for gratuities, and then the cruise line breaks it down between the various support staff who service you during the cruise.

Just like when you are eating out at a restaurant, tipping on a cruise ship is not required. And the daily per-person fee is a recommendation. If you do not feel you have received the service that would warrant a tip, you can get with the purser and modify the amount you would like to tip.

So, how is the tip broken down? Based on a $10-$12 per person per day rate, here is a typical breakdown:

- Cabin Steward: $3-4/day
- Dining Room Waiter: $3-4/day
- Maitre D': $0.50 - $1/day
- Head Waiter: $0.50 - $1/day
- Assistant Waiter / Bus Boy: $1.50 - $3/day

In addition to your room steward and dining staff, you will still have other people you may want to tip, like bartenders and wine stewards. When getting drinks at the bar, check your receipt, as most will already include a 15% tip. Feel free to add more for great service.

With spa services, the standard is 15-20%. Some cruise lines already include tips in their treatment price so be sure to check in advance. Tour guides receive a typical $2-3 to the guide and $1-$2 for the driver. Keep this in mind for some river cruises as well.

JUST ADD WATER

Some ships have a "Kid's Club." We don't have kids ourselves, but in talking with other cruise passengers we have heard that most people don't tip the kid's club staff—however, if you have a sick child or your kids had an amazing time, it would make sense to tip someone who has provided exceptional service.

On a river cruise, know that you will have a cruise director who is on call 24/7 to support you and help make your cruise enjoyable. This is another person you would want to tip generously.

Do not let the tipping part of a cruise scare you. Our general rule of thumb we follow is to pay the daily per-person rate and then give extra to our cabin steward, dining staff and bartenders who have helped make our cruise extra special. A good rule of thumb is to budget about 10% of your total cruise fare toward tips. Then again, it's your choice.

Medical onboard

You know the feeling, you begin getting those "something's not right" vibrations, or you start feeling like you are coming down with something. Mentally, you are fighting it. You're on vacation and you don't want anything to slow you down. Sadly, however, it does happen from time to time. The good news is, if you are on a cruise, they actually have a medical staff on-hand to help get you back in the saddle. You don't get this when you are on a land vacation.

Most of the large ships will have at least one doctor and a couple of nurses; usually more for the mega ships. Each of the medical staff members must have at least three years of post-graduate experience in general and emergency medicine. They can also be board certified in family, internal or emergency medicine.

If you do become ill or become injured, you can visit the ship's infirmary. It will most likely have regular operating hours, but if needed, there will be staff on call 24 hours a day for emergencies. They will have a limited pharmacy—most of the items they carry are for motion sickness, respiratory problems, or cardiovascular issues as well as some vaccines.

INSIDER TIP: Sometimes the motion sickness pills will be free of charge. And if the seas are really rough, you can also ask for them from the front desk.

Don't think the medical services are going to be free—you will receive a bill depending upon the type of service you required. Again, another reason to get your trip insurance or check your insurance policy to see what may be covered while you are traveling. It's always good to know in advance.

Amenities in Your Stateroom

The amenities in your room will vary between cruise lines, and also between stateroom categories within the same ship. For example, on *MSC Divina*, they have an exclusive group of staterooms called the Yacht Club. The Yacht Club is a "ship within a ship" concept. And the amenities in those staterooms are different than those found in the standard staterooms on the rest of the ship. On the Disney ships, each room has an empty small refrigerator whereas others will have a fridge stocked with mini-bar items.

We were thrilled when we went on a river cruise to discover they stock the room constantly with bottles of water. On the ocean-going ships, we bring on bottles of water or purchase a water package so we always have water in our stateroom.

Again, some lines offer cool amenities that you may fall in love with—then you go on a different line, and realize they don't offer those amenities. Check with your specific cruise line and cabin category to verify what you'll have in your stateroom.

Disembarking

One thing that surprises most cruisers is that they have to pack up their luggage and put it outside their stateroom for pick up on the last night of the voyage. This is to expedite the process of getting off the ship the next morning. Most people will do this. Just don't pack the items you will need to get dressed and ready the next morning along with your carry-off bag.

But you don't have to pack the night before if you plan ahead. Kerri and I bring luggage for the cruise that is easy to attach together like a train, so we can leave whenever we want, without having to check our bags, or use a porter once off the ship. Usually the people who carry off their luggage get to leave the ship first. If you have a bottle of wine or a chilled bottle of champagne (our favorite for this occasion) that you bought while in port, this is a great time for a final toast while most people are standing in line.

If you did put your bags out the night before, you will be assigned a number/color tag and will then get off the ship when that group is announced, pick up your bags and clear customs. It's all easy. This day will be the saddest day of your vacation.

CHAPTER EIGHT
PLACES TO SEE AND THINGS TO BUY

Always at the top of every list of why to cruise are the places you visit. Some of our favorite travel memories have been things we have done while cruising like the port stops on our Mediterranean cruise and the ancient cities in Southern France along the Rhone river. Places we will never forget, and still talk about.

Shore excursions fall into three categories.
1. Booked through the cruise line.
2. Booked through a third party company.
3. On your own.

There are reasons for each, so let's take a look here. If you book a cruise line excursion, you have more protection. What we mean is that if your excursion is running late, and the ship is scheduled to leave, the cruise line will wait for you in most cases. There is a connection between the company and the cruise line. Not the case if you book through a third party company. An example would be, if you called a charter fishing company directly and booked a fishing trip in the Caribbean. The cruise line doesn't know that you booked it, and that your charter may be late getting back.

As cruise lines start to offer shore excursions as part of all inclusive packages, sales for third party companies could drop. One main reason they exist is because typically cruise lines don't pay commissions to travel agents on shore excursions. We expect that to change as well.

On your own is just you and your friends getting off the ship and walking around town, or grabbing a taxi and sightseeing at your own pace.

If you are a first time cruiser, or the port is particularly exotic, you may want to book the cruise line options.

JUST ADD WATER

We have done all three kinds, and one of our favorites was when we had a limo driver in Tuscany that we arranged through our agent. He picked us up in a slick Mercedes van.

Our first stop was Siena. The heart of Siena is its central piazza called the Il Campo, known for its famous horse race, the Palio. If you have seen the James Bond Movie, Quantum of Solace, then you have seen the Palio. It's the opening scene of the movie. Hey, if it's good enough for 007, it's OK in my book!

After a self-guided tour of the city, we headed to a family-owned winery in Tuscany called Fattoria di Montecchio. We not only tasted a few wines, they also showed us the process of making olive oil. One of the reasons I still remember it so well is that it was just Kerri and me, and one of the family members who owned the estate. That's about as good as it gets for a tour, as far as I'm concerned. If you get a chance, definitely give it a visit.

The Caribbean is the best place for "on your own" excursions. There are always cab drivers all over the ports, and in most cases there is plenty to do within walking distance. If you are looking to shop or find the best place to eat and hang out, ask the cruise director or another crew member. They almost always know the insider shops, restaurants, and also the best place to get free wi-fi. In some cases, you can call an excursion operator directly and negotiate your own price. Just be aware of the refund and cancellation policy!

On many occasions we have just walked around the town, shopped, and had a few drinks. If it's your first time in the Caribbean, you may want to choose a few excursions in advance.

Where I don't recommend doing it on your own is in the Mediterranean or Alaska, unless you are experienced there. There is just too much to potentially miss if you're not familiar with the area.

The River Cruise difference. Don't like having tons of shore excursion options to sort through? Then river cruising may just right for you. Most river cruise lines have the excursions already included.

On some days you will do more than one. Some are at night, like our "Ghost Walk" tour in Viviers, France. Seeing an ancient city at night is a completely different experience than during the day. River cruising is so hot, it has its own chapter.

Shopping in Port

There are three times that you can buy things duty free: when you are flying internationally, when you are in a cruise port, and when you are onboard (as we previously mentioned). An important thing to know is the price of what you want to buy where you would normally buy it. If there are certain liquors that you like to drink, or to give as gifts, price them out before you go anywhere. What may look like a great deal, in fact, may not be one at all. Here are a few things on our list to buy duty free.

Liquor

On our last trip to Europe, we flew through Miami. We had just barely started our trip, and it WAS for business, and we bought some vodka and rum at the Miami airport. Of course we had to carry it in our luggage the whole trip (we may have to do that in reverse next time).

The Caribbean is famous for having great liquor, particularly rum. We toured the Bacardi factory in San Juan, and it was a blast. In almost every Caribbean port you will find great deals on all kinds of alcohol—just make sure you have a price at home to which to compare it.

Watches and Jewelry

I am a huge fan of watches, as you may now know. That alone should tell you what age range I am in. I do NOT use my iPhone to tell time. There are some great watch shops in port. If you know what you are looking for and have a price in mind, it will make shopping in port easier. Otherwise everything looks like a good deal and who wants to get home and realize you only saved $10 on a thousand dollar watch.

Perfume and Cologne

Again, the same rule here is to know the price of what you want to buy from your local store where you normally buy it. For these products, also make sure you are comparing apples to apples—meaning, bottles of the same size. I have found that the sizes of some fragrances in port are actually much bigger than what your local retailer offers, but it is the same price.

Electronics

One of the main reasons I avoid buying electronics in duty free shops is I want to be able to go to someone if it stops working. I buy almost all of my electronics at either Apple or Best Buy for the great service and extended warranties. For professional equipment for our TV show, we like B & H Photo. You may find some good deals. Just know ahead of time what you're looking for. We have seen some good deals on cameras and lenses.

CHAPTER NINE
GROUP & THEME CRUISES

Group cruises are my favorite. There is nothing like cruising with a group of people whom you already know. I have organized both charity cruises and business cruises, and they have something in common: the camaraderie of cruising with people who think alike. Just like you can find a festival, seminar or event on land for your interests, you can do the same when looking for a cruise. The following will break down some of the dynamics of the different types of groups that can range from just a few cabins, to whole ship charters. Speaking of whole ship charters…

Kerri and I are HUGE old movie buffs, and at some point just about every weekend we will be in front of the TV watching the Turner Classic Movie channel, or at least using the DVR to record our favorite movies. When we first learned that they were doing a classic movie cruise and that we could sail with Robert Osbourne and Ben Mankiewicz, we were psyched! Unfortunately, the first two times this was offered, it was not in our budget. When we found out they were doing a third one, we vowed to make a deposit no matter what the cost. Booking early, as you now know, lets you break up the payments over time, with no interest.

We were excited that we would be sailing with not only the TCM hosts, but Robert Wagner and Alex Trebek, screen legend Jane Powell, and child star of the 30's and 40's, Margaret O'Brien! Rick Baker, master make-up artist (American Werewolf in London, Michael Jackson's "Thriller"), and film noire expert Eddie Muller were also in attendance. We even got to do a whiskey tasting with actress Illeana Douglas of *Goodfellas* fame and granddaughter of screen legend Melvyn Douglas.

TCM chartered the newly refurbished *Disney Magic*. It's hard to explain how much fun it is to experience a Disney cruise with almost NO kids. I think there were less than twenty people on the whole ship under the age of 21. No lines for the waterslides!

After hearing that acting legend Ernest Borgnine (who sailed on TCM 2) had passed away, we knew we had to go to every one of these cruises that we can, because we know we will not have these screen legends forever, and this is the best venue to see and meet them. One reason is the limited number of people, and five days to see them, as opposed to many thousands of people in a short amount of time at land-based events.

Family & Friends

Cruising for a family reunion has become very popular and it's easy to see why. Usually a reunion is planned by someone who "volunteered" and who may have very little travel experience. Most likely it's the person in the family whom everyone likes. A group on most cruise lines is eight cabins. Pricing is going to be similar, but using a travel agent can get you things like an onboard credit, free specialty restaurants, or a bottle of wine. If you are the organizer, and you work with an agent, you may even go for free!

Affinity Groups (also disguised as Theme Cruises)

This just may become your favorite part of the book, because it's one way you can cruise for free. Whether you realize it or not, you are part of an affinity group. Think not? Here is a quick memory jogger: Do you...

- Play a sport?
- Go to church?
- Have a favorite band?

- Like fitness or yoga?
- Love wine and food or craft beer?
- Like to dance?
- Talk politics?
- Ride or like motorcycles?
- Watch movies?
- Belong to a college or high school alumni group?
- Have a passion for reading?
- Play any card games?
- Keep a scrap book?

If you answered yes to any of these (and I know you did) then you are part of an affinity group. Here is the great news. You can cruise FOR FREE, by getting a small group together for a cruise. Most cruise lines have a group policy called a TC, for tour conductor, where for every 16 people who pay, one person can go free. You only pay the tax and port fees. Which also means that for every 16 cabins, you get one cabin free. Now you not only go free, you can bring someone with you and be the hero! And if you aren't into getting a bunch of people together yourself, there are plenty of existing groups you can be a part of their group cruise. Similar to the TCM Classic Movie cruise we go to each

JUST ADD WATER

year. You've probably even heard of some popular group cruises. Your travel agent can help you find one as well.

The undisputed heavy weight champion of music cruises is Sixthman. If you hear someone talking about a music cruise, odds are they're talking about Sixthman. Imagine hanging out with a boat full of people who all enjoy the same music, bands, artists, etc. Great dinner conversation and people you'll think are really cool because you have a common interest. Here are just a few of the cruises Sixthman has done or are still doing:

- KISS Kruise - thekisskruise.com
- Alabama Festival at Sea
- Florida Georgia Line - fglcruise.com
- Simple Man - Lynyrd Skynrd - simplemancruise.com
- Kid Rock's Chillin' the Most Cruise - kidrockcruise.com
- The Rock Boat w/ Sister Hazel - therockboat.com

Another example of an affinity cruise is "Dancing with the Stars At Sea" aboard Hollard America. This group capitalizes on the very popular ABC TV show (another type of affinity group). Here is a quick rundown for the 2014 season, and I see no reason that it won't continue in future years. On these select cruises guests will have the opportunity to:

- Participate in complimentary dance classes based on dance routines from the show. This is a chance to learn the basics or new steps.

- Compete in the "Dancing with the Stars: At Sea" competition. Following an early elimination process, finalists will have the opportunity to take to the main stage with the ship's dance professionals. One "Cruise Champion" will emerge, based on the highest combined point total from a panel of three judges, as well as audience participation.

- At the end of October 2014, the Cruise Champion with the highest score from each ship will have an opportunity to perform as a finalist on the Champions Cruise in December 2014. Finalists, plus a guest, will be invited on a complimentary 7-day Champions Cruise to the Caribbean, where the 15 finalists will dance for the coveted mirror ball trophy and the title Holland America Line "Dancing with the Stars: At Sea" Grand Champion.

Sports Teams

You can always find some kind of sports fan groups onboard a ship. During a New Year's Eve cruise, we can tell you there were plenty of people watching the bowl games on the two-story TV screen while wearing their college team colors. Sports fans are a natural to get together for any reason and show team spirit. Why not on a cruise?

When we sailed on the *MSC Divina*, they had a "Baseball Greats" cruise. These cruises happen a few times a year and you can participate in an interactive Q-and-A session with the players, enjoy player-hosted trivia games, and a fun story-telling session in which the players share candid revelations about some of the "characters" of the game. There are also pitching, hitting, and defense strategy clinics, along with a passenger pitching contest. The host and MC for all of the onboard activities on each cruise is former Yankee star Stan Bahnsen. Other baseball greats include Ken Griffey Sr. and former Dodger Bill Russell. Go to MSCcruisesUSA.com for more details.

Cruising is a great way to raise money and awareness for your club, as well. This works great for church groups, service organizations, or charities. You can include an additional amount in each cruise fare that will go towards the charity. A cruise vacation and raising money for your favorite cause says everyone wins to me.

Business Meetings/Incentive Trips

Want everyone to show up at a meeting? Have it on a cruise. I can't tell you how many boring meetings I have attended all over the country. Whether flying or driving, hotel-based meetings are not my favorite, and here is a strange reason why. Because of the crowds at some meetings, in the thousands, I am stressed out about when and where to eat. The group gets dismissed for lunch all at the same time, and most hotel restaurants are not ready for the massive rush of people. If you go off property, how do you get there, and is everyone else going to do the same thing? And then what do you do at night? Again, it's stressful to try and make plans, grab a cab to go out, get a group to meet up, etc. Not true on a cruise. Cruise ships are MADE for this. And the best part is that meeting space is included AND some audio/visual, too. Several cruise ships offer very nice meeting rooms and boardrooms so if you are concerned about a professional, classroom-like environment for your training or seminars, a cruise ship can offer just that.

Chances are when you hold a meeting at sea, your attendance the next year will increase because you have created a memorable event. Land-based meetings can't even compare. You can only do so much to a hotel ballroom or convention center.

JUST ADD WATER

Want to get your company excited about increasing sales or productivity? Make the prize a cruise! They will remember the experience long after a monetary reward. I still remember a trip to Hawaii I won back in 2000, a sales reward from the alarm company I worked for. In 2007, I won a travel sales contest and the reward was a three-day Carnival Cruise. I worked harder for that three-day cruise than I did the trip to Hawaii. I know…I have no idea why either! It makes no sense, but that's how much I love cruising.

To make this work, it has to be an incentive, not a contest. Here is what I mean. A contest is "the first five people to hit X sales goal, get a cruise as the reward." An incentive is "anyone who hits X sale goal gets to go." See the difference? In the contest example, the mindset is "well so and so are always the top sales people, so they are going to get to go, but not me." With an incentive, everybody wins.

When done right, the incentive trip pays for itself. Everyone tries harder, total sales go up, and even the people that don't hit the goal, still end up making more sales than they normally would have. Of course, this example is based on sales, but other criteria can be used as well. It can even be a total company goal: "Hit this figure, and everyone goes."

What we do know is that when people hear cruise, they have a really good idea what they are winning, and get motivated. Land-based incentives still leave too much to the imagination and people find it harder to really visualize. And, if you do a side-by-side comparison, you will quickly discover a cruise will be ten million times less stressful and you won't be nickel and dimed all week like you easily can be when on land.

Group cruising is fun. It can start with just a few people and explode to thousands. Try it, we think you'll like it.

CHAPTER TEN

RIVER CRUISING

If you have heard of river cruising, odds are its because of Viking River Cruises. Brilliant marketing, and a strategic partnership with the Emmy Award winning PBS show *Downton Abbey* has helped to put river cruising "on the map." And it benefits not only them. In our opinion, it helps the whole industry, by making people aware of the category. We are huge fans of marketing that goes against the norm, and Viking does it masterfully. Their slogan "Spend Less Time Getting There, and More Time Being There" is not only genius, it very accurately describes the experience. And strangely enough, I didn't have to look it up. The phrase from that commercial has been drummed into my head for the last year or so on every TV station, both network and cable. As soon as I hear the commercial, without even seeing it, my Pavlovian response is "hey, that's Viking."

ROB & KERRI STUART

Docking in the heart of famous cities, sometimes more than one a day, and being able to walk right into town is an amazing thing to experience, and what river cruising really is all about. Expertly chosen shore excursions (most included in the cruise fare), English speaking guides and Quiet Vox headsets make it a truly immersive learning experience, regardless of which cruise line or itinerary you choose.

When looking at different cruise lines and ships to cover on our show *All Aboard TV*, we knew we had to go on a river cruise. That, and every travel agent we know saying "you have to try one." After talking with Diane and Kristin at AmaWaterways about our ideas for a new cruise show, we immediately knew they were a great fit. After a few conversations with Sach, their marketing director, he asked us "how would you like to shoot onboard the AmaDagio, which cruises the Rhone River in Southern France." Ummm…yes, please!

Our only prior trip to France was a ski trip to the Alps, so we were very excited to have an opportunity to see the Provence region up close and personal on a river cruise.

The people that sail on river cruises are not looking for "Broadway" type shows, casinos, huge pools, and kids activities. It's very much about soaking up the scenery, immersing yourself

JUST ADD WATER

in the local culture and experiencing the history of where you are traveling. As a matter of fact, there were no kids on this cruise. #winning

If you have the idea that river cruising is just sitting on the deck watching the cities pass by, you are in for a big surprise. To show you how shore intensive a river cruise is, we are sharing our itinerary from the cruise we took on AmaWaterways. If you really want to experience it, check out our show *All Aboard TV* (www.AllAboardTV.com). This is a seven-night cruise (or eight-days). If you do their pre- and post-options, it becomes a 14-night cruise (or 15 days).

- Day 0 – Travel Day, arrive early enough and you can spend an afternoon exploring the city.
- Day 1 – Embarkation, Arles. Arriving to ship in the afternoon, welcome dinner.
- Day 2 – Arles. Morning excursion options to visit Les Baux and an olive farm or "Impressionist Experience," which included touring the insane asylum where Vincent Van Gogh committed himself. After lunch on the ship, there was another Arles walking tour.
- Day 3 – Avignon with option of a walking tour and Papal Palace tour or visit Pont du Gard and Uzes. Viviers at night with a ghost walk tour.

- Day 4 – Viviers with a Grignan excursion and a truffle farm visit.
- Day 5 – Tournon – Chocolate and wine tasting, then traveling to Vienne for an evening on your own.
- Day 6 – Vienne walking tour and then traveling to Lyon for another walking tour
- Day 7 – Belleville – Beaujolais excursion
- Day 8 – Lyon – DISEMBARK and then cooking demonstration followed by the high speed train to Paris for optional post-cruise tours.

As you see, your days are pretty full on a river cruise. You don't have to go on all the excursions and can certainly just hang out on the ship or explore on your own. However, the cruise lines partner with great local guides. You also get to wear handy headsets so you can actually hear the guide with having to be right next to them.

Alcohol

Building on the above information, if you are walking through a cool city and find a certain local brew or wine that you like, you can buy it and bring it onboard. That's right. Bring what you want back onboard, and drink it at your leisure. There is no

JUST ADD WATER

"alcohol X-ray" as you arrive back on the ship. So take it back to your stateroom or the upper deck and enjoy.

Pre/Post Hotel Stays and Transfers

With a few exceptions (the Mississippi River, for instance) you will be flying internationally to get to your cruise, assuming you are coming from North America. Staying a few days both before AND after your cruise is very popular. We even met several people from Australia who were getting off our ship and going to another cruise—same cruise line, but different ship and itinerary.

A great thing about the pre- and post-stays, as well as the transfers, is that they are arranged by the cruise line, and a great chance to meet fellow cruisers before you go, or hang out after the cruise. I have never seen so many people bond so quickly as I have on a river cruise, and staying with them at the hotel beforehand makes it happen even faster. If you are not doing a pre-hotel stay, you may want to at least opt for the transfer from the cruise line. That way if something happens to delay your bus, the ship will wait. If you arrange your own transfer and there is a problem, you may have to catch the ship at the next port.

River Cruise Lines

Although there are many river cruise companies, these are the ones that cater primarily to the North American market.

AmaWaterways (www.amawaterways.com)
AmaWaterways is a beautiful line that is family owned. The average number of guests is roughly 150 (75 staterooms) with the exception of a few smaller ships with exotic itineraries in Asia and Africa. Here are a few fun facts:

- The only river cruise company that has an African safari river cruise. Jack Hanna (yep, the one you are thinking of) highly recommends this cruise as a great way to see African wildlife.
- First river cruise company to offer bicycles for guests to explore the towns.
- You can choose from 15 different ships in their fleet and they recently ordered two more ships to be deployed in 2015.
- They have itineraries in Europe, Russia, Vietnam/Cambodia, Africa, and Myanmar (Burma).
- Their first ship was the AmaDagio in 2006 but their history in river cruising goes back much, much further.

JUST ADD WATER

Like most companies in this category, they offer some amazing pre- and post-cruise options at luxury hotels in the cities you may fly into before/after your cruise.

Avalon (www.avalonwaterways.com)

Avalon Waterways is a luxury river cruise company, as well. Their tag line is "Legendary river cruises. Inspired design.^{SM}" Recently they launched the Suite Ships® of Avalon in Europe. These include spacious, innovative Panorama Suites^{SM} with unique Open-Air Balconies." That's a fancy way of saying floor to ceiling glass window that opens.

- You can choose from several ships in their fleet, with 13 in operation in 2014 and two new ships being added in 2015.
- They offer some of the largest staterooms in river cruising.
- You will find Avalon Waterways in Europe, Asia, South America (Amazon) and the US (Mississippi and Midwest Rivers).

Everything aboard is premium, both first class service and accommodations from your stateroom to the living areas and fine dining experiences and exclusive tours.

Tauck (www.tauck.com/river-cruises.aspx)

Tauck started as a Connecticut-based touring company, then expanded and started the river cruise line, Tauck River Cruising. It's a good fit because they are first a touring company, and river cruse itineraries are destination intensive.

Here are some of their features:

- All-inclusive (onshore and offshore dining, alcohol beverages, gratuities, pre- and post-hotel, transfers and shore excursions).
- Three cruise directors per cruise – this is really unique and ensures that each guest gets lots of personal attention.
- They have two classes of ships and each have just 115-130 guests per ship, much lower number than other river cruise lines.
- They offer unique onshore excursions including an exclusive dining experience off the ship to experience local history and cuisine.

They recently christened their newest addition to the fleet *ms Inspire*. This brings their total fleet to seven. We can expect to continue seeing Tauck bring their touring influence to the river cruising industry.

JUST ADD WATER

Uniworld (www.uniworld.com)

Owned by the same company that owns several four and five star properties including the famous Red Carnation Hotels, Uniworld is a one-of-a-kind experience. It is "the world's ONLY authentic boutique river cruise line™" and sails in Europe, Asia and Russia. When you step aboard a Uniworld ship you will feel like you are in a boutique hotel. Here are some fun facts:

- 21 ships in their fleet, and a new addition is scheduled for 2015.
- Offer over 40 itineraries and 500 departures annually.
- They have the only river cruise ship with a REAL fireplace.
- Their newest ships include marble bathrooms in every stateroom.
- They offer an Italian river cruise itinerary that sails out of Venice. No other river cruise line sails in Italy.

One of their exclusive excursions is a lighting ceremony at St Mark's Basilica in Venice, Italy. They have many ways to personalize your cruise vacation. Plus, Uniworld is an all-inclusive experience, which includes first class pre- and post-cruise accommodations. And with their six-star experience you can be confident everything from the service to the food to the excursions will be exquisite.

Viking (www.vrc.com)

They are known for their Longships which is a class of ships within their fleet of 52 ships. Yes, I said 52. They are even in the Guinness Book of World Records for "The Most Ships Inaugurated in One Day by One Company" – a total of 16 on March 18, 2014. Overall, their ships hold more passengers than other river cruise lines, and the rooms may be a little smaller.

The Viking experience really focuses on the destinations. Their cruises aren't completely all-inclusive but do include wine, beer and soda at meals and at least one complimentary shore excursion at the various stops.

Viking is also adding ocean-going ships to their fleet. Their first ship will launch in 2015 and is called Viking *Star*, to be followed by the *Sea* and *Sky*. They changed their name from Viking River Cruises to Viking Cruises in 2013 to reflect this change.

Try a Viking River Cruise, and you really will "See Things Differently."

INSIDER TIP: Pack good walking shoes. And read about the destinations you will visit BEFORE you go on your cruise.

CHAPTER ELEVEN
SOCIAL MEDIA & STAYING CONNECTED

Your first reaction may be "why would anyone want to stay connected?" I get it. Most people love that they are getting away from it all. If you have ever cruised before the days of the internet and cell phones, the idea of being able to use both on a cruise ship might make you scratch your head.

With the way new ships are being built, you can now stay connected almost as if you are at home. Whether that's a good thing or bad thing is up for debate. As of this writing the big news in cruising is the "smart ship" concept unveiled by Royal Caribbean on their new ship *Quantum of the Seas*. The ship will feature high speed internet, which, if you have ever tried connecting to a ship's connection, high speed would not be the phrase to use. Cruisers should be able to use services like Skype and FaceTime to stay connected with anyone in the world.

If you are reading this, then the odds are you have a Facebook account. Many of you also have accounts with Twitter, Instagram and Pinterest. As newer ships are being introduced, you will start seeing more internet options, and I think that is smart. One very good reason is so people can use social media to "advertise" about their cruise. They are building new ships with the internet as part of the build, as opposed to retrofitting existing ships.

When we sailed on the inaugural cruise on Norwegian *Breakaway* for travel agents and the media, they allowed people to access Facebook accounts for free. Hello free advertising—a lot of the people were taking pictures of the ship, and sharing them on Facebook. I know, because I was connected and sharing, too. Access to social media platforms will most likely become common, so users can share their vacations in real time.

If you are going to use your cell phone while in port, make sure that you check with your phone carrier for international rates. You can also plan ahead if you want to stay in touch by phone. Ask a crew member where the best free wifi locations are, and then use that to connect with whoever you need to. On our Caribbean cruise that stopped in San Juan, Puerto Rico, I was able to return a few client calls because San Juan is part of the U.S. After being out of touch for a few days, it was nice to see the familiar ATT signal light up.

INSIDER TIP: Change your outgoing voicemail message to let people know you are out of touch. I also set up my email with an out of office responder. Nothing like having someone mad at you because they reached out to you multiple times, not knowing you were out of town.

ROB & KERRI STUART

JUST ADD WATER

CHAPTER TWELVE

7 NIGHTS, 7 TIPS, $700 IN SAVINGS

I know. Catchy title right? The number should actually be much higher, but my editor is a genius, and I listen to him. Let's find out how.

#1 Use a Cruise Travel Agent

As you have probably noticed, this is hands down our number one tip of the whole book. It also tops the list of these seven tips, and is the key component of the other six. Travel agents are the first to know about specials and incentives and their entire job is to know the cruise industry. Believe me, there is a lot to know, and just organizing the information and sorting through the clutter can be a full time job. Save your time (and money) for something you enjoy, like taking a cruise, and leave the research to the pros.

#2 - When to Book

Although Wave Season, January - March, or Cruise Week, in October, are typically the best times to book a cruise, it's not the only time to get a good deal. Keeping up on the incentives offered during this time though is a great way to save money. At the very least, put a deposit down on a cruise you would really love to go on. If something changes, you can always cancel and get a refund per the individual cruise line policies.

#3 - How Far Out to Book

Like any good business, cruise lines want to get customers on the books as soon as possible. By booking far in advance, we recommend 12 - 18 months, you not only lock in the best price and have price protection, there may be incentives offered. Here are a few examples of those:

- Onboard credit (OBC) = $100 - $250 per cabin
- Free dinner for two at a specialty restaurant = $50 - $70

- Pre-paid gratuities = $140+ for two people
- Kids sail free = $200 - $300

Not bad for simply saying yes a little farther in advance.

#4 - Time Flexibility, When to Sail

The busiest time of the year is Christmas and New Year's, which shockingly have the highest pricing of the year. No way! Those cruise line accounting geniuses! I just checked pricing for two different cruise lines for a seven night December sailing. The price range? December 6th, $549 per person. December 28th, $1399 and $1499! That's $850 - $950 per person in savings!! Not to mention that the taxes on the Dec 6th sailing will be lower. When looking at dates, being flexible one to two weeks on either side of that date can save you hundreds.

#5 - Choosing a Cabin

The lowest price in any category is called a guarantee. Did you know that there can be five or more categories within an "inside" cabin? The same for ocean view and balcony cabins. I did a live search when writing this, just to make the point. On this seven-day Caribbean sailing, there were five different categories for an inside cabin. The price difference? From $779 to $949. That's a HUGE difference, $170 per person, for the same size cabin. Just a different location. And let's be honest here. If you are getting an inside cabin, it's based on price. Why pay $340 more for a better location? Combine this with the tips mentioned above, and the savings is well over $1000 already. So let's keep going…

#6 - Depositing a Future Cruise

If you have never cruised, you won't know about this. And if you have been on a cruise and didn't pay attention, now is the time. This is ONLY valid during your cruise. If you are enjoying yourself, and over 98% of people do, then you can put a deposit down on a future cruise with that cruise line. You don't need to know the sailing date, or even the ship. You just need to know you want to go again with this line. The benefit? You get an onboard credit on the cruise you are currently on! Not every line has this, so check with the cruise line.

#7 - Credit Card Programs

There are so many credit card rewards programs out there and they are constant changing. So, for this tip, we are just using our favorite one as an example, American Express. And specifically the cards issued by AMEX themselves, not their affiliates like Costco or Delta Skymiles. The best part of these programs is the free perks. As long as you use your card to book the cruise, you can get things like a free bottle of wine or champagne, dinner for two in a specialty restaurant, and an average of $300 per cabin onboard credit! Membership really does have its privileges! As usual, check with your agent for more details, and thanks for playing!

ROB & KERRI STUART

CHAPTER THIRTEEN
BON VOYAGE

If you have read this far, congratulations, and thank a teacher. If you skipped to this part of the book, shame shame.

The information in this book, while current at the time it was written, like most things, is not only subject to change, you can count on it doing so. As a matter of fact, things DID change as we wrote this.

Here are a few of them:

Celebrity announced their entry into river cruising via a partnership with "A Top Secret Company." Yes, we know… but if we told you…

RCI unveiled its "smart ship" concept for *Quantum* and *Anthem* that has some of the coolest things you could ever imagine for a cruise ship... like a robot bar tender, "smart" wristbands and true high speed internet.

Some lines are experimenting with all inclusive experiences, mainly drink packages and shore excursions. Expect this to continue as the demand for a "one price" vacation increases. MSC Cruises launched their "Experience Packages" with four options to choose from. The package you choose determines where your cabin will be on the ship, some extras that are included in that package (like drinks), and a few other perks for the higher end packages.

Expect more Cruise Line / Entertainment partnerships similar to Holland America and "Dancing with the Stars at Sea", and Celebrity and "Top Chef at Sea." These alliances bring awareness to both brands and is a true win-win.

As Viking has thrown down the virtual gauntlet in river cruise marketing, expect to see more from other lines like AmaWaterways and Uniworld.

To stay up with the latest happenings in the cruise industry, please follow us on Facebook, Twitter, Instagram and YouTube.

JUST ADD WATER

Here are the links to our sites. Click on them if you are reading this as an eBook. Do not click if it's a real book. Clicking on a real book does nothing, and makes you look silly!

Facebook: /AllAboardTV

Twitter: @AllAboardTV

Instagram: @AllAboardTV

YouTube: /AllAboardTVshow

Thank you for spending your time with us and we hope to run into you on a future cruise!

Until then, Bon Voyage!

Rob & Kerri

p.s. - If you DO see us on a cruise, come up and say "Hi." If you have a copy of *Just Add Water* with you, we will sign it for you, and then buy you a drink. Or, if you took our advice and bought a drink package, you can buy us one (subject to ONE drink per book.) Welcome Aboard !!

ROB & KERRI STUART

ABOUT THE AUTHORS

Rob and Kerri have been passionate about cruising since their first experience almost a decade ago. Since then they have sailed all three major cruise regions of the world on multiple lines. They turned that love of cruising into a travel agency, this awesome book, and a TV show, *All Aboard TV*.

When not cruising, they live in St Petersburg FL with their two fish, who, because of Rob and Kerri's busy travel schedule, do not have names.

ROB & KERRI STUART

JUST ADD WATER

WATCH US ON
ALL ABOARD TV

All Aboard TV is the first TV show dedicated 100% to cruising. All cruising, all the time. We invite you to join us as we explore various cruise lines and ships as well as ports and destinations visited by way of a cruise. Check out our channel and our shows:

All Aboard TV Features

Shoreside

Home Port

You can find us online at www.AllAboardTV.com, on a digital network (like ROKU) and on broadcast/cable channels in select markets.

ROB & KERRI STUART

YOUR CRUISE NOTES

JUST ADD WATER

YOUR CRUISE NOTES

ROB & KERRI STUART

YOUR CRUISE NOTES

www.ingramcontent.com/pod-product-compliance
Lightning Source LLC
Chambersburg PA
CBHW051944290426
44110CB00015B/2107